God from the
Machine

COGNITIVE SCIENCE OF RELIGION SERIES

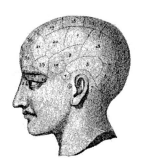

Series Editors: **Harvey Whitehouse**
and **Luther H. Martin**

The Cognitive Science of Religion Series publishes research into the cognitive foundations of religious thinking and behavior and their consequences for social morphology. The emphasis of the series is on scientific approaches to the study of religion within the framework of the cognitive sciences, including experimental, clinical, or laboratory studies, but works drawing upon ethnographic, linguistic, archaeological, or historical research are welcome, as are critical appraisals of research in these areas. In addition to providing a forum for presenting new empirical evidence and major theoretical innovations, the series publishes concise overviews of issues in the field suitable for students and general readers. This series is published in cooperation with the Institute for Cognition and Culture at Queen's University Belfast.

TITLES IN THE SERIES:

Modes of Religiosity
A Cognitive Theory of Religious Transmission
By Harvey Whitehouse

Magic, Miracles, and Religion
A Scientist's Perspective
By Ilkka Pyysiäinen

Why Would Anyone Believe in God?
By Justin L. Barrett

Ritual and Memory
Toward a Comparative Anthropology of Religion
Edited by Harvey Whitehouse and James Laidlaw

Theorizing Religions Past
Archaeology, History, and Cognition
Edited by Harvey Whitehouse and Luther H. Martin

How the Bible Works
An Anthropological Study of Evangelical Biblicism
By Brian E. Malley

God from the Machine
By William Sims Bainbridge

FORTHCOMING TITLES:

Mind and Religion
Psychological and Cognitive Foundations of Religion
Edited by Harvey Whitehouse and Robert N. McCauley

The Evolution of Religion
By Harvey Whitehouse

God from the Machine

Artificial Intelligence Models of Religious Cognition

WILLIAM SIMS BAINBRIDGE

ALTAMIRA
PRESS

A Division of
ROWMAN & LITTLEFIELD PUBLISHERS, INC.
Lanham • New York • Toronto • Oxford

ALTAMIRA PRESS
A division of Rowman & Littlefield Publishers, Inc.
A wholly owned subsidary of The Rowman & Littlefield Publishing Group, Inc.
4501 Forbes Boulevard, Suite 200
Lanham, MD 20706
www.altamirapress.com

PO Box 317, Oxford OX2 9RU, UK

British Library Cataloguing in Publication Information Available

Library of Congress Cataloguing-in-Publication Data

Bainbridge, William Sims.
    God from the machine : artificial intelligence models of religious cognition /
William Sims Bainbridge.
        p.   cm. — (Cognitive science of religion series)
    Includes bibliographical references (p.   ) and index.
    ISBN 0-7591-0743-2 (cloth : alk. paper) — ISBN 0-7591-0744-0 (pbk. : alk. paper)
        1. Religion and sociology—Computer simulation.   2. Psychology, Religious—
Computer simulation.   I. Title.   II. Series.
    BL60.B185 2006
    200.1′13—dc22

                                                                          2005024897

Printed in the United States of America

⊗™ The paper used in this publication meets the minimum requirements of American National Standard for Information Sciences—Permanence of Paper for Printed Library Materials, ANSI/NISO Z39.48-1992.

Contents

List of Figures and Tables

1

Simulation

In an often-told science fiction story, scientists build a huge computer and feed it vast amounts of information in order to answer the most profound questions about existence. As soon as it is finished, they turn it on and ask, "Does God exist?" The computer smugly answers, "I do now!" (cf. Brown 1954). This book has the more modest aim of using existing computers to explore the implications of ideas from the social science of religion in a new way.

Deus ex machina ("god from the machine") refers to an arbitrary means for escaping a difficult situation, as when ancient Greek and Roman theatrical melodramas hoisted an actor playing a god onto the stage by means of a derrick, to save the day for the hero. Petronius said, "Fear first brought gods into the world," and by this logic all gods are contrivances designed to rescue humans from an inconvenient reality. This book will not attempt to say definitively what gods actually are, because our focus is on human beings, particularly their beliefs and the social processes through which they acquire religious faith. Rather than introducing a god by means of a lifting machine, we use a computing machine to explore fundamental social processes of religion among humans.

Computer simulation has become a major tool of scientific research in fields as diverse as chemistry, physics, and economics. It is time for computer simulation to be applied to the scientific study of religion. It has already gained a foothold in adjacent disciplines; for example, simulation is widely used in the field of social networks (Smith and Stevens 1999), and networks are the basis of religious conversion and recruitment to religious movements. Because religion concerns private belief as well as group membership, we need a form of computer simulation that incorporates models of human minds.

Artificial intelligence (AI) is a well-developed field of computer science that models cognitive processes, and it is a major part of cognitive science. This book will employ two different but compatible forms of AI: rule-based action and neural networks. Rule-based reasoning is akin to formal logic; it models cognition as a series of if-then propositions connected through mental deductions (Kowalski and Levy 1996; Hopgood 2001). Here, we model the cognition socially, in what is sometimes call *artificial social intelligence* or ASI (Bainbridge et al. 1994).

Neural networks simulate the actual structure of the human brain, the connections between neurons or between assemblages of neurons that constitute mental associations, and are the basis for learning rules of behavior (Wasserman 1989, 1993; Hinton 1992; Karayiannis and Venetsanopoulos 1993; Kontopoulos 1993; Smith 1993; Schultz 2003; Quinlan 2003).

Already a standard research technique in economics, computer simulation has also gained a foothold across the other social sciences (Hanneman 1988, 1995; Gilbert and Doran 1994; Gilbert and Conte 1995). Religion is such a diverse collection of human beliefs and behaviors, and the social science of religion draws eclectically upon theories and methods from so many fields, that surely computer simulation will be valuable for exploring at least some issues. The aim of this book is to demonstrate that this new methodology need not be limited to peripheral issues, but is a valid and often powerful tool for exploring questions that are central to the scientific study of religion.

There is a widespread consensus that the approach used in this book, called *multi-agent systems* or *agent-based modeling*, is usually the best way to represent social interaction in computer simulations (Epstein and Axtell 1996; Macy and Willer 2002). An agent is an artificial intelligence computer program or software module that can take action in a larger computational environment, much as a human being might. A multi-agent system, as the name implies, consists of a collection of more or less autonomous agents that exchange information or interact with each other (Kaminka 2004). In a simulation such as those described here, each agent represents a person, and the total system represents a society.

Sabrina Moretti (2002, 46) predicts that multi-agent systems could have a profound influence on sociological theory, and addresses three related challenges. First, she writes, "theories of rationality need to be extended to learning and adaptation." In the context of the social science of religion, this relates directly to the new paradigm, sometimes called the *rational choice* approach (Jelen 2002), which is sometimes accused of relying too heavily upon rational calculation. Machine learning is currently one of the most active areas of artificial intelligence research, and adaptation is a hallmark of the comparable field of evolutionary computing. Thus a considerable toolkit of computational methods is ready to expand and deepen the rational choice approach.

Second, Moretti argues, multi-agent systems are an excellent medium in which to formalize the psychological theories on which sociological theories so often rest. Among others, the simulations described here incorporate Fritz Heider's Balance Theory, Gordon Allport's theory of cognitive effort, and the Stark-Bainbridge theory that religion chiefly concerns the exchange of general compensators that offset human frustration. The theories become formalized in the structure and specific instructions of the programming code through which the simulations are created. This book will not offer the source code, because it is not written for programmers but for students and social scientists of religion. Instead, the text describes the dynamics and results of the simulations that spring directly from the code, and the source code itself will be made available for those who might want to look more deeply into it.

Third, Moretti (2002, 46) says that formalization of knowledge is "one of the principal challenges in the development of multiagent systems." Of particular importance for us here are the kinds of knowledge people have about other human beings and about those transcendent beings they believe may exist, namely, the gods. The simulations described in chapters 2 through 4 of this book take knowledge essentially for granted, by modeling social decision-making processes for which the options are already defined. A hint of free will is modeled in these early simulations by means of random numbers that represent probabilities of making one choice versus another. Later simulations employ neural networks and related learning mechanisms to offer much more subtle models of knowledge, and we can hope that the developments going on even now in AI laboratories will give us even more powerful tools to model the discovery and application of knowledge in future years.

THEORIES OF RELIGION

One may ask why it is legitimate to model the transcendent spirituality of the human soul with a soulless machine. Of course, the answer depends to some extent upon whether one believes that humans have souls, and the evidence from contemporary cognitive science seems to be that they do not (Pinker 1997; Bloom 2004). Although some readers will argue that the "higher" mammals—apes, dogs, cats, and maybe horses—possess souls, few will say this about computers. When Tracy Kidder (1981) called his book about the design of a computer *The Soul of a New Machine*, presumably his metaphor referred to the spirit of the people who built it, not to the machine itself. However, many computer scientists and ordinary users take the phrase *artificial intelligence* seriously, believing that there are more similarities than differences between the functions of the human brain and those of a computer system.

According to psychoanalytically oriented sociologist Sherry Turkle, there have been at least two phases in the historical development of thinking about computer intelligence. In the early days of the 1960s and 1970s, most artificial intelligence programs followed rigid rules in a logical manner—such as sequences of if-then instructions. During that period, specialists and the general public alike might acknowledge that the machine had a kind of intelligence, but not the same kind as the human one. It lacked anything like free will or subtlety. Then, in the 1980s, approaches like neural networks and evolutionary programming (e.g., genetic algorithms) introduced a new kind of machine intelligence that possessed what Turkle (1995, 125–48) called *emergence*. The results are not programmed in and may not be predictable. Because the computer no longer operates "mechanically," one could say it is no longer a machine, in the traditional sense of the term, but an evolving information system at least somewhat analogous to the human mind.

I originally turned to computer simulations in 1983, as Rodney Stark and I were writing the pair of books in which we offered an outline of a general theory of religion (Stark and Bainbridge 1985, 1987). Our book *A Theory of Religion*, and the more recent excellent effort along the same lines by Stark and Roger Finke (2000), offered a number of formal propositions connected by verbiage arguing that some statements followed logically from others, but we lacked the means to be fully rigorous. It was difficult to see how we could develop a notational system or adapt the existing methods of symbolic logic to derive proofs about social behavior rigorously, so I sought other methods. I was aware that computers were being used to duplicate or even help originate mathematical proofs—probably the first example was the computer program Logic Theorist, completed in 1956 by Allen Newell, Herbert Simon, and J. C. Shaw (Crevier 1993)—so I decided to explore computer simulation. My first very simple simulations were published in the 1980s (Bainbridge 1984, 1985b, 1986, 1987); I occasionally applied the technique to the sociology of religion in the 1990s (Bainbridge 1995a, 1995b, 1997a), and then consolidated my preparation to write this more comprehensive work during two years serving as director of the artificial intelligence program at the National Science Foundation.

The formal name of the program I ran is Artificial Intelligence and Cognitive Science, and this multidisciplinary field of cognitive science has become increasingly important over the past 30 years. A number of cognitive scientists of both the psychological and anthropological persuasions have recently argued that religion is the natural result of the way the human mind works. On the basis of psychological and anthropological data, some have argued that the human brain evolved in such a way that people tend to see complex phenomena as the actions of conscious beings, thus encouraging belief in gods (Pinker 1997; Boyer 2001; Atran 2002; Barrett 2004). Research on both children and adults led Bloom (2004) to argue that humans imagine they have souls because the human brain has no awareness of its own functioning, and thus humans falsely perceive themselves to be separate from their bodies. Perhaps more controversially, Eugene d'Aquili and Andrew Newberg have argued that the module of the brain that defines a person's subjective boundaries can give a sense of fusion with a broader spiritual reality when it experiences sensory deprivation (d'Aquili and Newberg 2000; Newberg, d'Aquili, and Rause 2001).

I have not attempted to test these theories here, simply because the application of artificial intelligence techniques in the social sciences is not sufficiently advanced. We must walk before we can run. Indeed, cutting-edge work in AI has not yet been able to simulate full human consciousness with computers, and something like that may be required before we can model a mind that is aware of other minds. A rather different cognitive theory of religious experiences has been offered by Harvey Whitehouse (2004; Whitehouse and Laidlaw 2004; Whitehouse and Martin 2004) based on the distinction between *episodic memory* (of unique events, usually emotionally intense) and *semantic memory* (of general facts, based on repetition). Whitehouse suggests that the cognitive distinctness of these two kinds of memory supports two different styles of religion, comparable to the sect versus church distinction in modern societies. Computer science models of episodic memory seem to be advancing rapidly (Shastri 2001, 2002; Nuxoll and Laird 2004), so in the next few years it may be possible to simulate Whitehouse's theory with machines.

Computer simulations have many potential applications within the sociology of religion, whether they make use of AI or not. One that has already proven fruitful is extrapolating the rates of growth or decline of different denominations, or projecting memberships demographically on the basis of fertility and mortality trends in different populations (Johnson and Barrett 2004). The classic sociological questions explored in this book include outreach strategies, religious conversion, ways that faith may limit deviant behavior, competition between denominations in the religious marketplace, interfaith hostility, and perhaps most importantly, religious belief. From the standpoint of contemporary behavioral science, belief equals cognition. Whenever a social process or sociological theory can be stated rigorously, its dynamics can be modeled. Comparing the results of simulations with real-world data not only checks the programming but more importantly reveals how well we understand the phenomenon in question, because a carefully written simulation is only as good as the concepts through which it models reality.

One of the most significant scientific approaches to studying religion, namely sociology, has remained aloof from the development of cognitive science. This is doubly unfortunate, because many sociological theories are cognitive in nature, and because sociologists possess so much data about religious cognition, notably in hundreds of questionnaire studies of religious belief. One consequence is that cognitive scientists are likely to ignore some of the most relevant work in sociology, because it is not explicitly labeled *cognitive*.

A prime example is the work of my main mentor in graduate school, George C. Homans (1950, 1967, 1974), who liked to call himself a behaviorist. In psychology, behaviorism is seen as the opposite of cognitive science, and thus is abhorred by cognitive scientists. However, Homans emphasized forms of cognition such as the social exchange of approval for advice, and the abilities of humans to recognize similarities in complex situations. For him, behaviorism merely meant focusing on observable forms of behavior, rather than speculating about inner states without benefit of empirical evidence, as he believed too many sociologists did.

The work that Stark and I performed in developing a social-interaction theory of religion is both cognitive and readily simulatable. Like Homans, we argue that humans join together in groups in order to help each other obtain rewards (e.g., food) and avoid costs (e.g., dangers), sharing information as well as material rewards with each other. Where Homans wrote about advice, we refer to explanations about how rewards can be gained and costs avoided. When rewards are relatively unavailable, people often share explanations that are based on supernatural assumptions. This, we argue, is the origin of religion, although centuries are required for the emergence of formal religious organizations. Other writers may be correct that the human brain has a propensity to assume that complex events are the result of conscious agents, but that is not a sufficient explanation of religion. One also needs a theory that harnesses the human mind to developing full-fledged theologies and the social organizations needed to sustain them, and that is where our theory comes in.

This book is not, however, limited to the Stark-Bainbridge theory of religion, nor to the rational choice version of it that Stark and Finke have developed. That theory will feature very prominently in the concluding chapters of this book, but it does not dominate the entire effort. I employ other theories, some from outside the field of religion, and I seek to expand the scope of theories that do focus on religion. Importantly, as Moretti would have advised, I have programmed the simulated people not only to make decisions but also to learn from their experiences.

MACHINE LEARNING

Machine learning is an identifiable branch of artificial intelligence, employing a variety of computational methods. Both among behavioral psychologists and among computer scientists who specialize in artificial intelligence, the kind of learning employed in many of the simulations presented here is called *reinforcement learning* (Russell and Norvig 1995, 598–624). Another traditional term is *operant conditioning* (Skinner 1938). The agent behaves in a particular way. The result is either a reward or a punishment to some degree or other. The learning takes place when the computer program changes one or more numbers in its memory registers, to reflect the agent's gain or loss from the particular behavior. The result of the behavior is feedback that provides information that can be useful to the agent in guiding future decisions about how to behave.

The nature of beliefs is somewhat controversial within AI, and there are various ways of defining them (Perlis 2000). A subjective definition of belief is "what a person or artificial intelligence takes to be true." One problem of this definition is how we decide what the entity takes to be true. We cannot look inside the head of a person to see directly what he or she really believes, but must infer belief from behavior—including from the words the person speaks. In the case of an AI agent, however, we have two ways of examining belief: (1) indirectly by observing behavior, and (2) directly by looking at the contents of the computer memory registers where the agent's mind is stored.

The mind exists to guide behavior, so presumably comparing behavior with direct measures of belief will show a close correspondence.

In general, human beliefs are neither perfectly confident nor entirely consistent. Even the most extreme fanatic always harbors doubts. In any complex system of ideas, it is likely that some will contradict others. This is especially likely if the ideas were acquired through learning in a complex environment, as is the case for most ideas held by humans. With computers, there are various ways of handling uncertainty, notably statistical probabilities and fuzzy logic. In several of the simulations reported here, beliefs are represented by a pattern of numbers stored in memory registers. These numbers can be interpreted in two ways: (1) the probabilities that the agent will behave in a range of particular ways, or (2) the agent's estimates of the likely reward or cost it would experience if it did behave in each of these ways.

Imagine a hungry mouse in a very simple psychological experiment using a T-maze, as illustrated in figure 1.1. I published an AI program of this mouse nearly 20 years ago (Bainbridge 1986). If mice were capable of being religious, this mouse might pray for cheese. This very simple computer simulation is not meant to illustrate religion but very basic principles of machine reinforcement

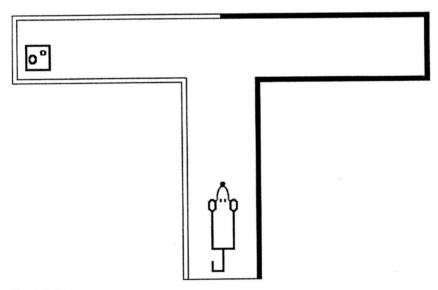

FIGURE 1.1
An Artificial Intelligence Mouse in a T-Maze.

learning. So all the mouse can do is scamper up to the branch point where it must turn either right or left. Assume the mouse cannot actually see the cheese at this point, but must make a decision based on its memory. But if this is the first time it has been in the T-maze, it has no memory and does not know where to expect the cheese, so it must choose at random.

Say by pure luck the hungry mouse goes left and finds the cheese. After it eats some, we put the mouse back at the bottom of the T-maze, and let it look for cheese again. On this second run, when it reaches the branch point, it does not simply remember where the cheese was and turn left again. Rather, it will have some probability of turning right, albeit a lower probability than it has of turning left. Animals and humans must behave in a manner that gains them not only material rewards but also information, so there must be a mechanism in the brain that allows the organism to explore new territory at least a small part of the time, even as it primarily exploits well-charted old territory (cf. Herrnstein 1971; Johnson 2002). As the mouse runs through the maze again and again, finding the cheese on the left each time, the probability it will turn right declines, and the probability it will go left increases but halts somewhat short of 100 percent.

Suppose we change the contingencies now, and put the cheese on the right. At first, the mouse will continue to turn left most of the time, but in fairly short order it will learn to turn right most of the time. Once it has learned a high probability of turning right, we could change the contingencies again.

In a moment, I will explain how to program a simulated mouse to behave in this somewhat subtle way, but first consider a simpler, less flexible, and frankly far less interesting approach. We could easily program the mouse to remember merely the last time it ran through the maze. The mouse has only one memory register, called WhichWay, holding only one byte of data: "L" for Left or "R" for Right. At random, we set the memory register at the beginning to "L" or "R."

Each time the mouse prepares to look for cheese, the computer looks in the memory register called WhichWay. In case it finds "L" there, it should make the mouse go left. Then the computer should check to see if there is cheese on the left branch of the maze. If it is true that the cheese is there, the mouse should eat some of it. If it is false that there is cheese on the left branch, the mouse should remember to go right next time. Similarly, if WhichWay contains "R," the mouse should go right. Again, it will either eat some cheese or, if it finds no cheese, it should learn to turn left next time, by putting "L" in WhichWay. This memory system has little or no growth potential, and it does not incorporate the probabilities of behavior we described above.

Now we shall rewrite the program procedure to handle behavioral probabilities rather than certainties. The key addition is a variable called Probability that stores a decimal number between 0 and 1, representing the probability that the mouse will turn left. The computer accomplishes the decision by generating a random number. The mouse would turn left unless the random number were greater than the probability of turning left, which is stored in Probability. This is just one of several ways of giving the mouse the remembered Probability of turning left.

Suppose the mouse does turn left. If it finds cheese, it will eat some of it, and the probability of turning left next time is increased, say, by 0.1. The maximum probability of anything is 1.0, so we want to prevent Probability from increasing above 1.0. We also want the mouse to have some chance of turning right, no matter how many times it was rewarded for turning left, so we set the limit of Probability somewhat below 1.0, arbitrarily in this program at 0.9.

The rest of the program code handles the three other cases, going left but finding no cheese, going right and finding cheese, and going right but finding no cheese. Finding cheese on the left, or not finding it on the right, increases the probability of turning left next time. Finding cheese on the right, or failing to find it on the left, reduces the probability of turning left next time, but limits are set to prevent the probability from reaching the extremes of 0.0 or 1.0.

This relatively simple program, based on repetition of rudimentary principles, allows the mouse to learn constantly, as reinforcement contingencies change, if it has only one choice to make between two alternatives. Now we can consider briefly one way of giving it a slightly more complex mind, capable of learning which of two cues to follow in deciding which way to turn.

Suppose we can illuminate one side of the T-maze or the other, distinguishing the two sides not in terms of Left or Right, but in terms of Dark or Bright. We, the omnipotent experimenter, can determine where the cheese should appear—Dark, Bright, Left, or Right. One way to program the mouse to handle this is to give it two probability registers: ProbabilityLeft and ProbabilityDark. Suppose the left side happens to be dark on the particular run, and the cheese is there. If the mouse goes left, the computer will increase both ProbabilityLeft and ProbabilityDark by 0.1. Suppose on the next run, the left side is bright, and there is no cheese. Then, the computer will *decrease* ProbabilityLeft by 0.1, but *increase* ProbabilityDark by 0.1. The mouse is learning to discount the left-right distinction and seek the cheese in the dark side of the maze.

With two competing cues (Left-Right and Dark-Bright), the mouse must have a way of deciding which one to pay attention to. One way to conceptualize this is that the mouse is developing a theory about the location of cheese that consists of two parts: (1) a category scheme, and (2) a location within the category scheme. As just described, the category scheme may be the distinction between dark and bright, and the location to expect cheese is Dark. Just as we used probability to decide which way the mouse would go, we can use probabilities to decide which category scheme it should use.

A successful theory will have a memory register with a probability number in it that is far from 0.5—perhaps as extreme as 0.1 or 0.9. An unsuccessful category scheme will not be able to distinguish the rewarding from the unrewarding direction to go, and will contain a number close to 0.5, which is the point of pure ambivalence. Thus, the mouse could compare ProbabilityLeft with ProbabilityDark and select the one that was further from 0.5. Or, to make the theory fully probabilistic, the computer could calculate how far each of ProbabilityLeft and ProbabilityDark was from 0.5, and select one with a probability proportional to its difference from 0.5 versus the difference from 0.5 of the other memory register.

In the concluding chapters of this book we will employ a much more complex memory system based on the same principles of reinforcement learning and probabilistic theories of reality to model the development of religious faith in human beings. The mouse described here is a very stupid machine, but it does learn. Although it has only two memory registers, they preserve the result of several experiences of scampering through the simple T-maze, and guide the mouse in making choices. Through some very simple programming, the mouse develops a theory about how to find cheese, and thus it exhibits rudimentary cognition. The theory tells the mouse which sensory cue to pay attention to, and it allows the mouse to predict where it will find cheese. Depending upon the magnitude of the probabilities, when the mouse selects a direction to go, with some justice we could say it had either hope or faith.

The environment the simulated mouse inhabits, the T-maze, is far too restricted for the simulations of human social behavior we need to perform, so a new and far richer environment is required.

OUR TOWN: CYBURG

The simulations we explore in this book will all take place in an imaginary big town or small city named Cyburg. Its population is exactly 44,100, a number chosen simply because it will be convenient for some of our simulations. Like all other numbers ending in double zero, 44,100 is evenly divisible by 100. This makes it possible to specify exactly what percentage of the town should belong to a particular denomination or religious movement in a given computer run. For some simulations, we might want to have a small number of different denominations of exactly equal size, and 44,100 is evenly divisible by all integers 1 through 7, plus 9, 10, 12, 14, 15, 20, and 25. Also, 44,100 is a perfect square, and for simplicity's sake the first simulations described in chapters 2 through 4 will imagine that the houses of Cyburg are arranged in a square, 210 homes on a side.

More importantly, 44,100 is in a good range, large enough so that one resident of the town could not possibly know all of the others, although residents might know everybody in their immediate neighborhood. Much of the research on social networks and on social exchange has unfortunately involved very small numbers of people. For example, the famous Bank Wiring Room studied by Rothlisberger and Dickson (1939) and explicated by exchange theorist Homans (1950, 48–80), included just 14 people. This was just barely large enough that the social network had two distinct cliques, but far too small to show social structure on many different levels. In Cyburg, we can focus on a small neighborhood or friendship clique if we wish, but we also can expand our view to encompass a widely extended social network and multiple subcultures. As Granovetter (1973; cf. Watts 1999) showed, it is often important to look at extended social networks. Two people who are strangers to each other may be linked through intermediary relationships with others—friends of friends, and the like.

Also, a somewhat large number helps us with the edge factor. Suppose our town had only 64 houses, arranged as on a chessboard. Then, nearly half of the residents (28 out of 64 or about 44 percent) would live on the edge of town, with fewer next-door neighbors than the others. With 44,100 residents, 836 live on the edge, but this is only about 2 percent. On the one hand, 836 is a large enough number that we could explore the implications of living at the edge of town with a sufficient number of cases for reliable statistical analysis, but in most simulations we can ignore the edge effect because it involves only a tiny fraction of the town's population. It would be possible to have the computer "wrap around" the location of the houses, so the town actually had no edges, but this would have the science-fiction effect of creating a town in the shape of a donut and thus make it hard to conceptualize as well as faintly ridiculous. The geographic shape of the town is actually relevant only for some of the simulations, especially the earliest ones.

The population is big enough that the results of a single computer run are not generally dominated by random factors, unless some interesting social process gives chance some leverage. Yet it is small enough that today's computers can process many steps of each simulation in the blink of an eye.

Cyburg is in the population range of several real cities that were the focus of classic social-scientific community studies. When the Lynds studied "Middletown" in 1925, it had 36,500 people and 42 churches (Lynd and Lynd 1929), somewhat smaller than Cyburg. A decade later, Middletown had grown to almost 50,000 with 65 churches (Lynd and Lynd 1937), somewhat larger than Cyburg. When Warner and Lunt (1941) studied "Yankee City," it had 17,000 people. "Hilltown," a Massachusetts town made sociologically famous by Homans (1950, 334–68), based on dissertation research by D. L. Hatch, had a population in 1945 of only 1,019. Cyburg's range is large enough to study not only competition among several denominations but also to chart the growth of a social movement, as William Sheridan Allen (1965) did in his study of "Thalberg" in Germany, which had a population of exactly 10,000 in 1930.

THE CHAPTERS AND THEIR SIMULATIONS

Chapter 2 explains how and why we do computer simulations, and it introduces some of the methods that will be used throughout the book. It draws upon work by Thomas Schelling, who proposed an extremely simple game to illustrate how social segregation can emerge through the decisions of individual people, even if none of them actually wants the segregation to occur. First, we imagine that Cyburg has two religious groups—such as Protestants and Catholics in Northern Ireland—who are somewhat suspicious of each other but not deeply hostile. Then we look at situations like Lebanon or Sudan where there are three or more distinct religious groups involved in the process of social segregation and conflict.

Chapter 3 looks at how new religious movements can spread through a social network, still employing very simple methods of simulation. The social-science literature of innovation diffusion often assumes that some people—called *early adopters*—are different from others in their greater willingness to try new things. The first simulation discussed in this chapter questions whether we need to assume that some individuals are religious early adopters, in order to explain much about the changing rates of diffusion of new religious movements. Related simulations explore how a movement can achieve faster success through concentration of forces—bringing extraordinary recruiting efforts to selected nonmembers in order to overwhelm their doubts—and trace the gradual triumph of one denomination over others as the result of pure chance.

While maintaining the same clear model of Cyburg, chapter 4 introduces more complex multirule reasoning systems to show how religious conversion and recruitment to religious movements actually occur in the real world. The different rules are major classic theories from social science: Edwin Sutherland's Differential Association Theory, Heider's Balance Theory, and the 7-step theory of religious conversion of Lofland and Stark. The computer software allows the researcher to combine theories, to compare how they affect the growth or decline of religions, and to evaluate the patterning of denominations across the society.

Chapter 5 introduces the first, simple neural network technology—the Minimum Intelligent Neural Device, or MIND. Again, residents of Cyburg who belong to various denominations interact with each other, learning to trust or distrust each other. This simulation models thought processes involved in interfaith relations, based on Homans's theory of interaction and Allport's theory of prejudice. Fundamental to this chapter is the fact that humans learn from experience but have limited capacity to abstract correct rules from their experience. MIND was specifically designed to be a neural network that could solve complex problems but also make mistakes, such as becoming prejudiced against some people because it fails fully to understand the social situation.

Chapter 6 concerns the basis of morality, which is cooperation. In an extremely influential rule-based simulation study, political scientist Robert Axelrod showed that cooperation could arise in human society even without shared values, culture, and religious commandments or ethics. Building on Axelrod's rule-based approach, this chapter examines how religion may nonetheless promote morality. The citizens of Cyburg interact with each other, making agreements to exchange rewards. Some people keep their promises, whereas others violate them. Persons follow one or another of a set of cognitive strategies for dealing with this perplexing situation. On the level of the entire community, this provides the basis for the emergence of morality—or its failure to emerge if conditions are not propitious. Importantly, the simulation explores how membership in religious communities may facilitate cooperation among members.

Chapter 7 focuses on the mental processes people experience when they develop religious faith. Interacting with other human beings in a search for material rewards, humans also want eternal life and other practically unattainable rewards. As they learn how to gain rewards from fellow humans, they generalize from this exchange to imagine supernatural beings—similar to humans but vastly more powerful—from whom the most valuable rewards might be gained. Thousands of simulated human beings, their minds modeled by somewhat complex neural networks, interact and learn cognitive maps of their social territory that depict not only the other people in Cyburg but also supernatural beings. This simulation draws on the Homans's classic exchange theory (1950, 1974), and springs directly out of the theory of religion of Stark and Bainbridge (1985, 1987).

The final chapter employs the most fully developed version of the simulation, but it also loops back to the beginning and links later findings to earlier concepts. Partly based on models of cult formation, and on general sect theory developed by many writers in the sociology of religion, this chapter explores how religious movements of many kinds tend to emerge in society. The model includes such features as family religious traditions, social class differences in sectarianism, and charismatic leaders. It suggests that many of the key concepts from the scientific study of religious movements and of denominations can be derived from fairly simple cognitive processes and fundamental principles of interpersonal communication.

2

Segregation

This chapter illustrates how and why we do computer simulations, and it introduces some of the methods that will be used throughout the book. It draws upon work by economist Thomas Schelling, who proposed an extremely simple game to illustrate how social segregation can emerge through the decisions of individual people, even if none of them actually wants the segregation to occur.

The simulations described here introduce several ideas that connect artificial intelligence to traditional social-scientific concepts. Notably, they illustrate some of the most rudimentary concepts of rule-based AI. Sociology has long postulated that people often follow rules governing behavior, namely, *norms*. The rules in this simulation are more like what economists call *preferences*, and they concern the conditions under which a particular person might feel satisfied or dissatisfied. A dissatisfied person is motivated to take action, if the option presents itself to become more satisfied. These rules are principles of decision making.

In the simulations described in this chapter, and those in the third chapter as well, my programming told the simulated people what rules to follow. True individual *artificial intelligence* comes later, when the simulated people are complex enough for what we call *machine learning*. However, this chapter will introduce the beginnings of *social cognition*, an implicit thought process carried on above the level of the individual, either in the group or the society as a whole, the fundamental principle of *artificial social intelligence* (Bainbridge et al. 1994). If *neural networks* are a good way to model individual intelligence, then *social networks* are a good way to model social intelligence. The individual agents in ASI are the social equivalent of the neurons (nodes or units) in neural networks.

SUSPICION AND SEPARATION

History affords many examples in which different religious groups coexisted in a situation of tension that occasionally boiled over into bloody conflict.

Perhaps the classic case was the battle between two groups separated literally by one iota of difference. Edward Gibbon commented long ago that "the profane of every age have derided the furious contests which the difference of a single diphthong excited between the Homoousians and the Homoiousians" (Gibbon 1896/1776–1788, vol. II, 352), while acknowledging that the theological differences between the two were in fact substantial. In our own era, we are painfully aware of the tensions between Protestants and Catholics in Northern Ireland, Jews and Muslims in the Middle East, or Muslims and Hindus in Kashmir. In other cases, the conflict may involve 3 or more groups, such as Muslims, Christians, and Animists in Sudan, or Christians, Muslims, and Druze in Lebanon.

We will begin to explore such tensions with the example of Northern Ireland in mind. Despite the history of violence, there are real connections between the two communities, and people of good will on both sides. Probably most people in both groups wish the tensions would go away. Although there are real sources of conflict, whether rooted in history or in group competition for economic resources and political influence, there are also factors bridging the social gap and offering reason for optimism. However, the sheer existence of a religious divide can increase the probability of conflict, and contribute to the growth of hostility borne of suspicion.

To begin with, we will imagine that Cyburg has two religious groups—Protestants and Catholics, as in Northern Ireland—who are somewhat suspicious of each other but not deeply hostile. Each individual may be willing to live near a member of the other group, so long as the other group does not dominate the neighborhood. Collective action is far more than just the sum of individual action. The behavior of one individual can take on an entirely new meaning in a particular social context. The behavior of a person can have unintended consequences, especially in interaction with the behavior of other people.

Social separation often has very significant consequences. When Catholics and Protestants have frequent interactions with each other, they come to know each other as individual people, having a realistic perception of the good and bad in each individual. They come to rely upon each other for certain rewards—whether through buying and selling goods and services to each other or through informal exchanges in which each person is directly valuable to the other. Constant contact provides information, and in many situations it brings the realization that the other group really is not a threat. As Homans repeatedly commented, people who interact frequently will tend to like each other and to become alike (Homans 1950, 1974).

Separation, in contrast, breeds distrust. Indeed, prejudice may be a consequence of segregation, as much as a cause. People fail to benefit from interactions with members of the other group, so they do not value them as sources of rewards. Catholics and Protestants may come to define themselves and the other group in terms of the most visible differences between them— such as being "papists" or "Bible-thumpers." Separation transforms personal identity, potentially increasing the tendency of an individual to think of himself as essentially a Catholic versus a Protestant, rather than as a Christian who happens (perhaps merely by reason of family tradition) to attend a Catholic or Protestant church. The individual reacts to a member of the other group as an outsider, alien, estranged. Once a line between them has been drawn, the groups will compete for political power and economic status. Religion will become implicated in many of the other conflicts that exist in the particular society. This particular simulation does not model all these consequences of segregation, but later simulations will return to such issues.

THE LOGIC OF SEGREGATION

In his 1978 book, *Micromotives and Macrobehavior*, economist Thomas Schelling asks us to imagine a neighborhood of 64 houses, arranged like the squares in a checkerboard. Initially, we can think of it as a small part of Cyburg, a mere one-seventh of 1 percent of this metropolis, and then later we can expand our thinking to the whole town. Schelling imagined that the inhabitants belonged to two social groups in the abstract—whether different races, political parties, or religions did not matter. Here, we will think of them as Protestants and Catholics. A third of the homes are occupied by Protestants, a third by Catholics, and the final third are not occupied and thus available for someone to move into them.

Consider one of the Catholics; call him Andrew. His immediate neighbors are 3 Protestants and 1 fellow Catholic. Perhaps he has no real hatred of Protestants, and would be happy to have one or two living next door. But he and the other Catholic are outnumbered in their immediate neighborhood, and it makes them uncomfortable to be in the minority. Figure 2.1A shows Andrew's neighborhood at one point in time, whereas figures 2.1B and 2.1C show the

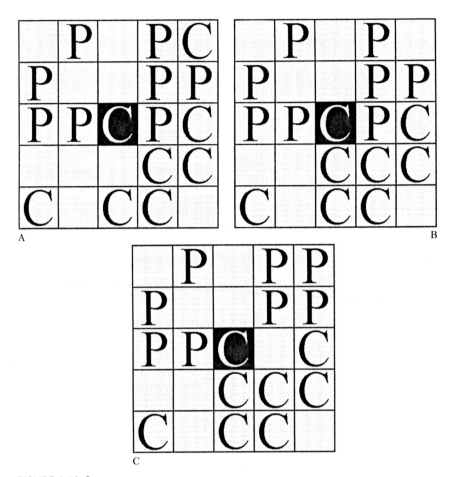

FIGURE 2.1A-C
(A) Catholics Are a Minority in Andrew's Neighborhood; (B) Catholics Are Equal with Protestants in Andrew's Neighborhood; (C) Catholics Are a Majority in Andrew's Neighborhood.

same area at two later points in time, which we will discuss momentarily. Each square represents a home, and the letters P and C represent Protestants and Catholics.

The computer defines a person's neighborhood as the person's own home plus the 8 homes that surround it. Thus, figure 2.1A is centered on Andrew, whose home square is colored black to identify it. Immediately around him, we see 3 Protestants and 1 other Catholic. So the totals in his immediate neighborhood are 3 Protestants and 2 Catholics. In the illustration as a whole, there are 8 of each denomination, but only the nine squares at the center count as Andrew's neighborhood.

If Andrew is following the decision rule to avoid being outnumbered, then he clearly is dissatisfied, because his denomination is a minority in his own immediate neighborhood. His one Catholic neighbor, living in the square below and to the right of Andrew, is in a different situation, however. That Catholic has only 1 Protestant neighbor but 6 Catholic neighbors (counting Andrew), so if he is following the same decision rule, he (unlike Andrew) is satisfied.

Andrew, being dissatisfied, will look for an opportunity to move to a different home where he would be satisfied. On his turn, he consults the real estate listing of vacant homes, selects one at random, and checks it out to see if he would be satisfied. In the real simulation, that prospective home could be anywhere in Cyburg, but for sake of this exposition we will limit ourselves to homes that are shown in the diagram. Suppose Andrew randomly selects the house just above his in the diagram. He imagines what it would be like if he lived there. Unfortunately for him, that house is practically surrounded by Protestants. If Andrew lived there, he would be the only Catholic and would have 5 Protestant neighbors. Clearly, that would not be an improvement. He would still be outnumbered. So, Andrew decides not to move, and he will not get another chance until his next turn.

Let's say the next person who gets to decide is the Catholic in the upper right square, with 3 Protestant neighbors. We don't know who lives above this Catholic, or to the right, beyond the edge of the diagram. But let's say this Catholic is outnumbered by Protestants and is interested in moving. He goes to the real estate listing and randomly selects a house. By chance it happens to be the one immediately below Andrew's home in the diagram. There, the Catholic would have just 2 Protestant neighbors and 4 Catholic neighbors (including Andrew). So the Catholic would be satisfied in that home, and promptly moves. Figure 2.1B shows the same area after that Catholic moved next door to Andrew.

By chance, Andrew gets a turn next. He used to be dissatisfied, but after the Catholic moved next door, he now tallies his neighborhood and finds there are 3 Protestants and 3 Catholics (including himself). So he is now satisfied, and does not check out a possible new home or consider moving.

Now, again by chance, the Protestant living to the right of Andrew gets a turn. In this person's immediate neighborhood there are 3 Protestants (including himself) and 5 Catholics (including Andrew). Feeling outnumbered, he checks the real estate listing and finds the house in the upper right corner of the diagram, recently vacated by a Catholic. He determines that he would be satisfied there, so he moves, producing the situation shown in figure 2.1C.

Andrew is still satisfied, but now Catholics are the majority in his immediate neighborhood—3 against 2. Andrew did not set out to live in a majority Catholic area. He merely did not want to be part of an outnumbered minority. Checking all 5 people living in Andrew's immediate neighborhood—the people for whom we can see all the near neighbors—we find that all of them are satisfied. Each of the 5 is a member of the majority denomination in his or her own near neighborhood, although each would have been happy if Protestants and Catholics were equal in number.

In the simulations to be described below, we will actually explore the implications of four different decision rules. A person could be satisfied with

1. One's own denomination not being a minority
2. A majority of one's own denomination
3. A plurality of one's own denomination
4. No members of other denominations at all

The first of these is the one we have been discussing. When there are only 2 denominations, the second and third rules are the same. A plurality is the largest of 2 or more denominations, whereas a majority means more than half. That is, with 3 or more denominations, a majority can be bigger than a plurality. Finally, there is the most hostile rule of all: avoiding members of other denominations altogether.

UNINTENDED RELIGIOUS SEGREGATION

For the first simulation, I set Cyburg to have equal numbers of Protestants and Catholics—14,700 of each, plus an equal number of empty homes to which they could move. Where the people live was determined entirely randomly by the computer across the square of 44,100 homes. But once it had assigned all the houses, I saved the arrangement, so I could call it up for reuse by later simulations. Given the equal numbers of Protestants and Catholics, we would expect about 50 percent of near neighbors to be of the same denomination, and indeed the actual figure happens to be 50.33 percent.

I set the satisfaction rules so that each group would be happy if its own denomination were not a minority in the immediate neighborhood. That is, a Catholic would be happy if he and his Catholic neighbors outnumbered his Protestant neighbors—or even if they were equal in number—just so long as they were not outnumbered. Following this principle, 74.34 percent of the 29,400 residents of Cyburg were satisfied, 74.57 percent of the Protestants, and 74.10 percent of the Catholics. This difference, of course, is the result of pure chance.

When the simulation runs, it goes through a series of turns, like many board games. Again and again, it would select one home at random, see if there was a resident, and then determine if he were satisfied. If so, nothing would happen. If, however, the resident were not satisfied, the simulation would check a list of unoccupied homes (the real estate list, if you will) and look at one vacant house selected at random. It would determine whether the dissatisfied person in the first house would become satisfied if he were to move to the vacant home. If so, he would move, and his old house would be added to the list of real estate vacancies. If not, he would stay where he was, continuing to be dissatisfied. The computer would do this again and again, 44,100 times, a cycle I call a turn.

Note that this is a little different from board games, because the random selection of homes does not ensure that each person actually will have a chance to move each time. Some will have multiple chances, but these will tend to equalize out over several turns. If the rules and the practical situation in the town permit, this process can be run until everybody is satisfied, and nobody moves any more. Table 2.1 shows what happened on each of the 21 turns required to achieve complete satisfaction in the first run of the simulation.

Table 2.1 shows that Cyburg was able to achieve 100 percent satisfaction in both groups, in exactly 21 turns, with 8,768 moves. If we ran the simulation again, with exactly the same initial religious geography, we would get a similar result, but the random selection of homes would probably require either more or fewer moves, and the simulation would end either earlier or later than the 21st turn. We see that most of the action takes place during the first 2 turns, and 99 percent satisfaction is achieved on the 7th turn. The remaining 14 turns are required merely to give the last, dissatisfied 1 percent a chance to find more satisfactory homes.

The major result of the simulation, and the reason Schelling proposed games like this, is the high level of segregation at the end. When the simulation began,

Table 2.1. People Moving to Avoid Being Outnumbered

Turn	Segregation (Neighbor Same) (%)	Total Moves	Percent Satisfied	
			Protestants (%)	Catholics (%)
0	50.33	0	74.57	74.10
1	61.01	3,705	87.08	87.20
2	67.24	5,572	92.28	92.16
3	71.09	6,630	95.05	94.91
4	73.65	7,318	96.65	96.60
5	75.36	7,800	97.84	97.75
6	76.48	8,116	98.62	98.49
7	77.16	8,323	99.07	99.86
8	77.73	8,488	99.37	99.35
9	77.98	8,565	99.59	99.55
10	78.24	8,636	99.73	99.66
11	78.40	8,680	99.84	99.76
12	78.49	8,704	99.86	99.84
13	78.54	8,720	99.89	99.90
14	78.60	8,737	99.89	99.93
15	78.62	8,745	99.93	99.95
16	78.65	8,754	99.95	99.97
17	78.66	8,758	99.96	99.99
18	78.68	8,763	99.99	99.98
19	78.68	8,765	99.99	99.99
20	78.69	8,766	99.99	99.99
21	78.69	8,768	100.00	100.00

about half of near neighbors belonged to the same denomination, which means that the other half of the near-neighbor pairs involved one Protestant and one Catholic. But by the time all the residents have become satisfied that they are not outnumbered, this measure of segregation has risen to 78.69 percent. That is, most near neighbors are of the same denomination, and only 21.31 percent of near-neighbor pairs have a Protestant living next to a Catholic. The residents of Cyburg did not intend to segregate their town, but by following their individual desires simply to avoid being outnumbered, they unintentionally achieved a substantial degree of segregation.

Nearly three-quarters of the members of both groups were satisfied at the beginning, and only one quarter dissatisfied. Thus, the segregation of Cyburg was accomplished by a minority trying to avoid being a minority. If there were 8,768 moves, then at least 20,632 people never moved at all. I say "at least," because some people may have moved more than once. A person's degree of satisfaction can change when somebody else moves in or out of his neighborhood, in search of his own satisfaction, as happened for Andrew in our original example.

EXTREME RELIGIOUS SEGREGATION

Having seen what can happen when a very mild concern about another group unintentionally causes segregation, we should now look at the opposite end of the hostility scale, when every member of each group intentionally wants to get entirely away from the other group. We should be prepared to find irony at this end of the scale as well. For the second simulation, I called up the same residential pattern as the first simulation, with the same number of Protestants and Catholics, but I set the decision rule differently. Now, a person will be satisfied only if none of his near neighbors belongs to the other group.

The degree of segregation begins exactly the same, again 50.33 percent, but certainly not the level of satisfaction. Where before nearly three-quarters of each group was initially satisfied, now only 4.14 percent of Protestants and 4.23 percent of Catholics are satisfied. Thus, there are powerful, majority urges to become segregated. Table 2.2, however, shows they have great difficulty achieving it.

As before, the simulation began with a significant number of moves, and some improvement in satisfaction, but this time it stalled and nothing happened after turn 12, even when I ran it all the way to 100 turns. At the end, less than 10 percent in each group was satisfied, compared with 100 percent in the previous simulation. Perhaps even more surprising, the final level of segregation

Table 2.2.   **People Moving to Avoid the Other Group Altogether**

Turn	Segregation (Neighbor Same) (%)	Total Moves	Percent Satisfied	
			Protestants (%)	Catholics (%)
0	50.33	0	4.14	4.23
1	52.34	753	7.07	7.25
2	53.33	1,092	8.36	8.61
3	53.83	1,257	9.01	9.33
4	54.08	1,335	9.37	9.65
5	54.20	1,377	9.50	9.81
6	54.25	1,393	9.62	9.88
7	54.26	1,400	9.65	9.90
8	54.27	1,400	9.67	9.91
9	54.29	1,410	9.69	9.94
10	54.29	1,411	9.69	9.94
11	54.29	1,411	9.69	9.94
12	54.29	1,412	9.70	9.94
...				
100	54.29	1,412	9.70	9.94

wound up much less—54.29 percent compared with 78.69 percent—even though the residents of Cyburg had wanted to achieve it.

The reason could be described in terms of a roadway traffic concept: *gridlock*. At the end, there were still 14,700 available homes, but each one had at least one Protestant and one Catholic living next door, so nobody was willing to move into it. Economists might call this a *coordination problem*. In principle, Protestants and Catholics could have negotiated with each other to divide the town by some "green line"—reminiscent of the line between Greek (Orthodox) and Turkish (Muslim) residents of Cyprus. One shudders to think of the carnage if they adopted the bloody method of separation that divided Muslims from Hindus when Pakistan and India were formed. But so long as the residents of Cyburg were limited to peaceful, individual decision making only, they could not do this.

PATH DEPENDENCE

We can take the irony to a higher, and possibly more realistic level, by allowing the simulated people to change their decision rules in midsimulation. Earlier we noted that segregation can stimulate suspicion and thus increase the forces working in the direction of further segregation.

The third simulation begins after turn 10 of the first simulation. I had saved the data, and simply reloaded it. At that point, more than 99 percent of both groups were satisfied, and the segregation had increased from 50.33 percent to 78.24 percent—nearly the 78.69 achieved at the end of the first simulation. Recall that the decision rule had been to stay in a home if one's own group was not outnumbered. I changed the rule so that people would no longer be satisfied with equal numbers in their neighborhood, but wanted to be a majority. They were still perfectly happy to have some members of the other group as neighbors, so long as their own group outnumbered them. This caused satisfaction to drop from over 99 percent to around 93 percent, as shown in the first row of table 2.3.

Then, as shown in table 2.3, I ran the simulation for 10 turns following the new rule. Segregation increased from 78.24 percent to 86.44 percent, meaning that at the end of turn 20 only 13.56 percent of near-neighbor pairs brought a Protestant together with a Catholic. Then I switched the satisfaction rule to the harsh desire to avoid the other group altogether, and satisfaction dropped to 58.23 percent for Protestants and 58.04 percent for Catholics. Thus by this

Table 2.3. **People Moving with Increasingly Hostile Decision Rules**

Turn	Segregation (Neighbor Same) (%)	Total Moves	Percent Satisfied	
			Protestants (%)	Catholics (%)
10	78.24	8,636	92.55	93.20
11	80.62	9,485	95.23	95.42
12	82.27	10,102	96.72	96.79
13	83.45	10,517	97.71	97.54
14	84.24	10,803	98.24	98.12
15	84.97	11,060	98.76	98.62
16	85.49	11,254	99.12	99.01
17	85.81	11,370	99.27	99.31
18	86.09	11,464	99.49	99.50
19	86.28	11,534	99.65	99.58
20	86.44	11,599	58.23	58.04
21	90.81	13,668	68.85	68.82
22	93.24	14,912	75.52	75.44
23	94.93	15,822	80.44	80.51
24	96.02	16,434	83.83	83.99
25	96.91	16,958	86.78	87.01
26	97.50	17,316	89.00	89.15
27	98.02	17,645	90.90	91.18
28	98.38	17,892	92.42	92.56
29	98.67	18,078	93.69	93.73
30	98.92	18,245	94.76	94.78
...				
75	100.00	19,052	100.00	100.00

point, a majority of residents of Cyburg already had no immediate neighbors from the other religious denomination, even though they only wanted to be in the majority in their neighborhood.

Another 10 turns brought Cyburg to the brink of total segregation. Fully 98.92 percent of near neighbors were of the same faith. Among Protestants, 94.76 percent had no Catholic neighbors, and thus under the harsh decision rule were satisfied. And 94.78 percent of Catholics had no Protestant neighbors. Running the simulation onward, gradually moves continued until perfect satisfaction and perfect segregation were achieved on the 75th turn.

It is interesting to note that if I changed the rule back to wanting merely to be the majority, or merely wanting to avoid being outnumbered, nothing would happen. The sequence of decision rules invoked in the simulation is like a one-way valve or a ratchet; it will go in one direction but not the other. This illustrates the fact in real human life that once segregation has occurred, it can be very difficult to undo it. Strict public policies, or a very long period of random moving, would be required to reverse segregation completely.

Of possibly great intellectual significance is the observation that Cyburg became segregated through a series of stages that needed to occur in about the given order. This is sometimes called *path dependence*, the phenomenon when the nature of the outcome depends very much on what route was taken to arrive at it. Decades ago, Homans (1967, 96–102) distinguished *divergent phenomena* from *convergent phenomena*. He wrote, "In divergence, a force weak in itself but just tipping the scales in a balance of stronger forces has big and spreading effects over time" (Homans 1967, 97). A convergent phenomenon is one in which the same destination might be achieved by many routes. Thus, divergence is another way of conceptualizing path dependence.

In social science, we tend to think that the "law of large numbers" swamps individual behavior, and in Cyburg the population is certainly large enough to overwhelm a single agent's action, under most circumstances. But in later chapters we will see a number of occasions in which a divergent phenomenon gets loose in the town, and an insignificant difference at time 1 becomes a huge difference at time 2.

SOCIAL GRANULARITY

One of the many buzzwords in computer and information science is *granularity*, the degree of detail at which information processing is done, or the size level at which data are aggregated. In religion, we know that congregations can be small or large, as can denominations. In measuring both, we tend to miss the smallest units, which, however, can be numerous. In my research on new religious movements, I am sure I have encountered dozens of one-person denominations, individuals who had their own self-crafted religion but no followers, and I have seen several examples of couples. In more conventional religious territories, there are analogies in unchurched individuals, couples, families, and friendship groups that share religious beliefs and practices, without belonging to any chartered denomination. Below a few hundred members, such community-based churches may not show up in official records or religious censuses.

Official lists of denominations, such as given in the *Yearbook of American and Canadian Churches* (Lindner 2004) and the historic censuses of American religious bodies, reveal a small number of very large denominations and increasingly greater numbers of smaller ones. The same general pattern is often called Zipf's Law and has been found for towns or cities and for corporations

(Zipf 1949; Axtell 2001). Incidentally, Zipf based his own theory to explain the distribution on a principle of cognitive least effort. We should examine the granularity of the third simulation, to have a perspective on the fine social structure of a fully segregated Cyburg.

Protestants are now completely separated from Catholics, but this does not mean they are in two separate areas of town. There are many unoccupied houses that can serve as buffer zones between many congregation-like social groups. I built many analysis tools into the software, including one that finds all the contiguous groups of each denomination and counts their population sizes. At the end of the simulation that produced complete segregation, there were fully 414 socially isolated groups. The three largest Protestant congregations had 1,139, 1,415, and 3,592 members. The three largest Catholic congregations had 1,471, 1,791, and 3,260 members. At the opposite end of the granularity scale, 64 people had no near neighbors at all, 28 Protestants and 36 Catholics.

Of the 414 congregations, small groups, or isolated individuals, fully 367 had fewer than 100 members. A total of 41 had more than 100 but fewer than 1,000 members. The 6 "large congregations" mentioned in the previous paragraph had more than 1,000 members each. Calculated differently, a total of 5,388 people belong to the smallest groups, those under 100 members. The middle-sized groups include 11,339 members, and the 6 very large ones have 12,673 members. The middle and large groups seem to me roughly the right magnitude to represent the actual 47 congregations of a real town of 44,100 people, and the remaining 5,388 people could be the unchurched members of both religious traditions. After all, the simulation had specified there would be only Protestants and Catholics, not atheists in town.

Of course, the real social structure of religious communities is the result of a tangle of complex factors, many of which have been identified by social scientists. However, it is always instructive to see what simple rules plus random variation can accomplish. Many structures in nature and society can be explained in large part simply as the natural result of random processes of aggregation, rather than either conscious design or some higher-level principle of organization. This is a key insight of the general simulation field sometimes called *chaos and complexity* or *self-organizing evolutionary systems*.

It may be helpful to see the kinds of granularity we are talking about. Figure 2.2A shows an area near the very middle of Cyburg after turn 10 of the first simulation—the same arrangement with which the third simulation began.

Figure 2.2B shows exactly the same area after turn 75 had produced complete segregation. This area of 441 houses, or exactly 1 percent of the total, contains quite a range of group sizes. Inspection of the two pictures suggests that several people did not move, and indeed since just 10,416 moved in the entire town between these two moments in time, one would estimate that only about 35 percent of the people in any such area would have moved by the end of the tenth turn.

In figure 2.2A, we see significant groupings of Catholics with Catholics, and Protestants with Protestants, but the 2 denominations have not yet completely

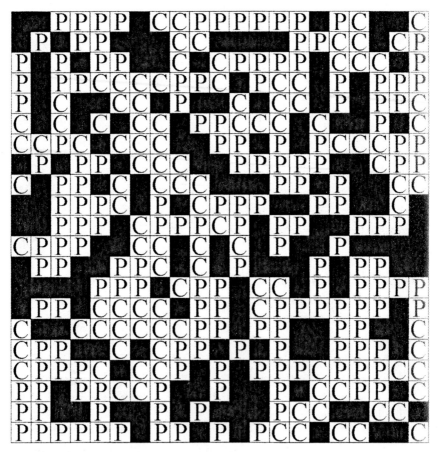

FIGURE 2.2A
Turn 10 of the Complete Segregation Simulation.

separated. In figure 2.2B, no Catholic lives next door—horizontally, vertically, or diagonally—to a Protestant. We can see spaces where 2 groups of one of the denominations could become united, if more of their coreligionists moved into the neighborhood. But not all of the groups of either denomination could be entirely connected without violating the preference against some member living next door to a member of the other—unless they can connect outside the square of 441 houses. Despite all the empty homes represented by black space, in neither diagram could a member of a third religious tradition move in without living next to either Protestants or Catholics.

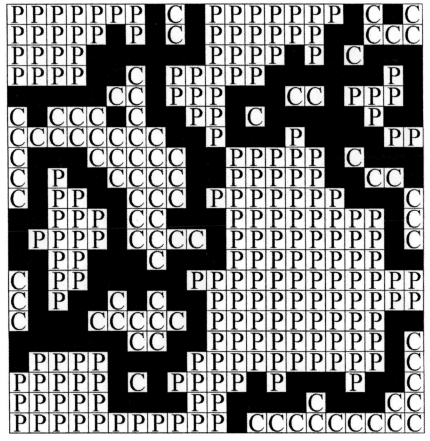

FIGURE 2.2B
Turn 75 of the Complete Segregation Simulation.

RELIGIOUS DIVERSITY

To this point, we have imagined that Cyburg possessed only 2 religious groups, Protestants and Catholics. It will be instructive to see what changes when we relax this assumption, and allow 3 or more denominations into the town. We will compare four different situations in terms of their initial and final degrees of segregation, and the results are only moderately different, so for sake of reliability we will do 25 runs of each simulation and report the averages. We will continue to have 14,700 empty homes and 29,400 people, but the number of denominations will vary from 3 to 10. For comparability, all the people will follow the decision rule from our first simulation. That is, each group would be happy if its own denomination were not a minority in the immediate neighborhood. In each case, we run the program until all residents achieve satisfaction, and we look at the degree of segregation that results.

In the first simulation of this set, we divide the population into 3 equal groups, giving us 3 denominations with 9,800 members: Baptists, Catholics, and Methodists, let us say. When we started with 2 denominations, in table 2.1, the segregation index (percent of near neighbors who are the same denomination) was 50.33 percent. Now, with 3 denominations, the average starting segregation (over 25 computer runs) is just 33.28 percent. Indeed, by chance we would expect about 33.33 percent. So, even before we start the simulation, we see that increasing the number of denominations reduces the segregation.

After completing the 25 runs with these conditions, the average segregation becomes 70.28 percent—also less than the 78.69 percent at the end of table 2.1, but considerably more than the 33.28 percent with which this simulation began. Thus, Schelling's irony holds up for 3 denominations, as it does for 2: People may create segregation without really intending to, if the actions of individuals to avoid being outnumbered cause them to move away from members of other denominations.

The second of these simulations keeps the Baptists and Catholics at 9,800 members each, but divides the third group into 2 denominations of 4,900 each; call them Methodists and Episcopalians. Even though 2 denominations remain at 9,800 members, splitting the other group into 2 denominations reduces the initial segregation, from 33.28 percent to 27.74 percent. (Again, averaged across another 25 runs.) The final segregation is also slightly lower, 66.67 percent.

The third simulation in this set continues to have 9,800 Baptists and 9,800 Catholics, but divides the remainder into 4 denominations of 2,450 members each: call them Episcopalians, Methodists, Lutherans, and Presbyterians. Again, the average initial segregation is reduced by adding denominations, now dropping to 25 percent, and final segregation drops slightly to 64.01 percent. However, the rise from 25 percent to 64.01 percent is a huge jump that more than doubles segregation—a factor of more than 2.5 in fact.

Finally, I ran a simulation 25 times with fully 10 denominations, all the same size, which means that each had 2,940 members. On average, each of these runs began with a segregation measure of just 10 percent, but ended at 52.21 percent, more than 5 times as great. Consider this 52.21 percent another way, in terms of Andrew the Catholic and the chances that a particular neighbor will be Baptist. Any given neighbor of Andrew has a 52.21 percent chance of also being Catholic. The remaining 47.79 is divided equally among the other 9 denominations, so the chance that a given neighbor of Andrew is a Baptist is just one-ninth of this or 5.31 percent. For a town with 10 equal denominations, therefore, 52.21 percent is a very substantial degree of religious segregation, even though the initial degree, 10 percent, seems objectively small. Thus, increasing religious diversity reduces segregation but does not eliminate a social process that increases segregation.

DECISION RULE VARIATIONS

The last of the new topics we will consider in this chapter is the fact that religious groups may differ in their feelings about each other. That is, they can have different decision rules or situations that they find satisfying. Earlier, we changed the rules during a simulation, but used the same rules for the denominations. Now, we will do 4 simulations, each with 3 denominations—call them Catholics, Methodists, and Baptists—but varying rules across denominations.

For the first of these simulations, I let the Catholics be satisfied unless they were outnumbered in their immediate neighborhoods, and at the start 65.03 percent of them were indeed already satisfied. But I let the Methodists be satisfied only if they were a plurality among near neighbors—more numerous than either other group—and only 45.20 percent of them were initially satisfied. I set the Baptist's rule even more stringently, letting them be satisfied only if they were a majority in their neighborhood, outnumbering both the Catholics and Methodists together, and only 28.67 percent of them were initially satisfied. At the start, the segregation measure was 33.43, but by the end, when everybody was satisfied, it had risen to 80.75 percent.

The first time we ran a simulation with 3 denominations, earlier, we had them all follow the mild rule of not wanting to be outnumbered, and they reached satisfaction with a segregation of 70.28 percent. Now we have achieved 10 percentage points higher with a mixture of decision rules. It would be wrong to say that the result of different rules across the groups will be a simple average of what would happen with those rules singly, but clearly the rules followed by different groups do combine to produce a distinctive result.

For the 3 other simulations in this set, each time I set the Baptist decision rule very stringently, letting them be satisfied only if none of their neighbors were Catholics or Methodists, and I varied the rules for these two other groups among less stringent alternatives. In the second simulation, both Catholics and Methodists were set so they would be satisfied unless outnumbered by members of another group. About two-thirds of the Catholics and Methodists were satisfied at the start, but among the poor Baptists only 0.90 percent were satisfied. Segregation began at 33.38 percent and rose for about the first 100 turns, at which point all of the Catholics and Methodists were satisfied, but only 20.68 percent of the Baptists. To make sure the simulation had really ended, I ran it to 1,000 turns, and nothing more happened. The Catholics and Methodists were unwilling to move to make room for Baptists, and the latter could not find any pure Baptist enclaves to move into. Segregation ended at 57.46 percent.

The next simulation was the same, except I changed the Catholic rule to being satisfied only if their own denomination were larger than either of the others in the neighborhood. This also reached gridlock when all Catholics and Methodists were satisfied, but with somewhat higher segregation (64.35 percent) and higher Baptist satisfaction (29.43 percent).

In the last of these varied rule simulations, I kept the Catholics and Baptists the same as the previous time, but set the Methodist rule so they would be satisfied only if they outnumbered both the other groups put together in their neighborhood. Again, the simulation reached gridlock with perfectly satisfied Catholics and Methodists. The final segregation was even higher (73.98 percent) and more Baptists were satisfied with the result (42.54 percent). This last set of experiments shows we can actually learn interesting things by giving different decision rules to the denominations. Here, we have seen that the fates of the Baptists were largely determined by the preferences of the two other groups, a social outcome if ever there was one.

SUMMATION

Religion is a social phenomenon. We cannot understand religious behavior merely by examining the motives and isolated actions of individuals. What one person does has implications for what the others experience, and thus for what they will do. In later chapters we will model how one person's beliefs interact with those of other people. Our approach is always social, but it also takes the individual human being as its fundamental atom of analysis.

What happens in Cyburg is entirely the result of the actions of individuals, but the results are more than just the sum of individual actions. Through interaction, people's behavior takes on new meanings and produces new consequences. There is no mystery about how these group-level consequences can emerge from individual behavior, but the consequences are not merely contained in the individual actions. Thus, there are two chief lessons of simulations like the ones discussed in this chapter:

1. We can understand much about religious social phenomena by analyzing them in terms of individual human beings interacting with each other.
2. In a social system, what happens is often more than just the sum of individual behavior, and one must seek special principles to understand how religious movements arise out of the actions of persons.

For Raymond Boudon, who introduced Schelling's simulation idea to sociology, this illustrates a social process he calls *magnification*, which may manifest itself in a wide variety of real situations. The social structure—the system of interactions and relationships that links individuals—transforms individual beliefs, desires, and behaviors. As Boudon puts it, "We are dealing here with structures where the interdependence between the agents has the effect of magnifying disproportionately their objectives" (Boudon 1981, 83). Perhaps religious intolerance may really be increased (if not actually caused) by processes of interaction in which the relatively moderate desires of individuals produce consequences that none of them might have chosen consciously.

It is normal for people of shared faith to flock together, and we can also read from these simulations some clues about how congregations and religious movements form and consolidate their social structures. Our simulation has imagined that people are actually moving from one house to another, quite a lot of effort if all they want to do is change their social environments. Alternatively, people can stay where they are, and reach out for their friendships beyond the immediate ring of 8 houses around home. In the next chapter we will look at a very different set of alternatives, the possibility that a person might change denominations, either converted by a religious movement or to conform to the modal denomination of their neighbors. To this point, religious change has all been external to the individual, seeking a fresh environment, but now we must begin to consider religious change that takes place within the individual.

3

Recruitment

Conversion to a religious movement or to a fresh religious affiliation for the individual has been a well-studied topic in the sociology of religion, and reasonably well-worked-out theory has been available for many years. Thus it will be useful to consider some of the classic theories in this chapter, both to render the computer simulations more intelligible and to anchor the artificial intelligence innovations of later chapters in existing scientific knowledge about human behavior.

THE LOFLAND-STARK MODEL

The classic theory of conversion to deviant religions was proposed four decades ago by Lofland and Stark (Lofland and Stark 1965; Lofland 1966; cf. Bainbridge 1978; Richardson et al. 1979). Although designed on the basis of observations of recruitment by the Unification Church in California, it was not really developed to explain a particular case but is an eclectic collection of ideas that were popular across sociology in explaining deviant behavior, including participation in social movements. This 7-step model claims to follow a value-added conception (Smelser 1962), in which each step must apply, in the order given, before an individual will join a radical group. However, it could just as easily be seen as a loose collection of factors, each of which increases the probability that a person will do so. According to the model, for conversion it is necessary that a person

1. experience enduring, acutely felt tensions
2. within a religious problem-solving perspective,
3. which leads him to define himself as a religious seeker;
4. encountering the group at a turning point in his life
5. wherein an affective bond is formed (or preexists) with one or more converts;
6. where extracult attachments are absent or neutralized;
7. and where, if he is to become a deployable agent, he is exposed to intensive interaction.

This chapter and the next will focus especially on the last three steps, whereas later chapters will consider ideas like those expressed in the first four. The early steps prepare an individual to accept new commitments by eroding his connection to old ones. The concluding steps employ social influence to establish the new commitments.

The first step, *enduring, acutely felt tensions*, addresses the motivation a person might have to abandon his current affiliation and adopt a new one. In a word, it concerns *frustration*. This frustration may have many causes—poverty, powerlessness, lovelessness, low status—but amounts to a felt discrepancy between the life the person has and the life he feels he ought to have. In the early 1960s, it was widely believed that a person would not violate conventional norms unless experiencing unendurable frustration in satisfying fundamental human psychological desires (Merton 1968; Dollard et al. 1939; Cohen 1955; Cloward and Ohlin 1960). The sociocultural turmoil of the 1960s, felt very powerfully within sociology itself, raised doubts about whether conventional society really could be taken for granted. In the chaotic, modern world, it may actually be the case that people are only very loosely tied to any kind of moral order, and very little may be required to liberate them from those vestigial ties.

Frustration may impel a person to take a big leap into the darkness, abandoning conformity for unconventionality. But this may not be necessary if conformity has become problematic in the society, as may be the case if traditional norms have already eroded society-wide or if the person's immediate social environment is already disorganized (Durkheim 1897/1951; Thrasher 1927; Faris and Dunham 1939). In terms of religious conversion, frustration may be required for a member of a conventional church in a traditional community to join a radical religious movement. But if the person lives in an area where cults are commonplace, proverbially such as Southern California, no frustration may be needed because no normative barriers need to be overcome. Alternately, conversion from one conventional denomination to another may not require any frustration, because such a lateral conversion does not require the person to increase his or her deviance with respect to conventional religious standards.

Enduring tensions constitute a problem the person faces that has resisted normal attempts at solution for some time. Culture can be seen as a more or less coherent bundle of solutions for problems, but it is not uniform. In modern societies, people are offered many different potential solutions for their emotional problems, including prayer and going to a minister for spiritual support and guidance. Lofland and Stark argued that many people have such a *religious problem-solving perspective.* If an unhappy person had instead a psychiatric problem-solving perspective, he or she might seek psychotherapy. A person with an educational problem-solving perspective might seek training in new skills, to build the basis of a better life perhaps through getting a new job. If traditional religious culture is strong in the society, many people will have a religious problem-solving perspective, and when their current religion does not solve their problems, they will become *religious seekers* in search of a new religion.

The fourth step in the model, *turning point,* is really the pivot on which the others turn. A turning point may mean a time in life when the individual is conscious that new lines of action are needed, and thus it may merely sum up the tension, problem-solving perspective, and seekership of the first three steps. Or, it could reflect the fact that a person's old commitments are coming to an end, including his ties to people of the past, thus marking a fresh openness for new attachments to new people. In terms of the deviance sociology of the 1960s, it invokes *control theory,* the view that a person will be free to deviate from conventional norms when his ties to society or the moral order are especially weak (Hirschi 1969). The three concluding steps in the Lofland-Stark model concern the interplay of social interaction that delivers the individual from one religious affiliation to another.

In the 1970s, sociology began to consolidate the ideas produced by the creative exuberance of the 1960s, and at the end of that decade, Stark and I suggested that social influence processes could entirely explain conversion to religious movements (Stark and Bainbridge 1980a, 1985). We were not claiming that frustration, culture, or other factors were really of no importance, but we suggested they should be ignored for the time being to see how much could be explained by the dynamics of social networks alone. Thus, we were proposing a research tactic—see how far you can get just with theories of social influence—that I will follow again in this chapter and the next.

UNOPPOSED RECRUITMENT
In the classic model of diffusion proposed by Elihu Katz and Paul Lazarsfeld (1955) and extended by Everett M. Rogers (1960), an innovation catches fire among so-called *innovators* or *early adopters,* people who are unusually ready

to try something new. These may be people who have felt enduring, acutely felt tensions in the Lofland and Stark sense, but they also could be respected opinion leaders in the community who have the social and material resources that make it easy for them to take risks. For example, a rich person can afford to buy a new product, at relatively low cost with respect to the person's entire wealth. Then, he transmits the innovation to other people, who are not so ready to try things without the recommendation of a trusted associate.

Classic diffusion theory has become well entrenched in business-related social science, for example, in textbooks on consumer behavior and marketing. In detail, this material differs significantly from what one generally sees in the sociology of religious recruitment, yet for two reasons I suggest the two separate literatures need to be brought together. First of all, the fundamental social mechanisms concern diffusion of innovation in general, not restricted to either the commercial or the religious realm. Second, the recently influential *rational choice* approach to religion, suggested by Stark, Finke, Iannaccone, and other colleagues, considers religious groups as if they were firms in a market, so principles of consumer behavior and marketing should apply (Stark and Finke 2000; Jelen 2002).

In these business-related textbooks, a sociogram was often included to show the principle of influence patterns across a network or the famous Katz and Lazarsfeld two-step model of opinion leadership (Kassarjian and Robertson 1981, 321, 351). Typically, consumers were conceptually divided into five categories in terms of how readily they accept new products: innovators, early adopters, early majority, late majority, and laggards (Rogers 1995). These five groups may be attributed contrasting personal characteristics: venturesome, respectable, deliberate, skeptical, and traditional (Kassarjian and Robertson 1981, 352). While widely accepted today, this model rests on questionable assumptions, and only certain parts of it are actually supported by careful empirical research.

One important aspect of this common model that can be evaluated by means of computer simulations is the explanation of the curve of diffusion. If one graphs the number of people who have adopted a new product over time, one often gets an approximate *logistic curve* that rises slowly at first, gaining momentum, rises rapidly for a while, then slows down again as the innovation approaches complete saturation of its prospective market. This is the so-called *sigmoid* or *S-shaped curve*.

Or, if one graphs the number of people adopting the innovation per time period, one gets an approximate *normal curve* (bell-shaped curve) that rises from zero with increasing speed, then slows down as it approaches its maximum, falls slowly at first, then more rapidly, then slowly at the end when it is back down near zero again. A sigmoid is simply the integral of a normal curve.

The normal curve is greatly responsible for the five categories of adopters, which are defined statistically in terms of standard deviations above and below the mean. The early majority and the late majority are one standard deviation before and one standard deviation after the mean time of adoption of the innovation. The early adopters are the second standard deviation before the mean, while the innovators are those more than two standard deviations before the mean. Standard deviation, of course, is an abstract mathematical concept that need not have anything to do with really distinct characteristics of the individuals, and it is a very poor basis for categorizing them. The five groups are entirely conceptual, and in this respect the traditional model of diffusion can be highly misleading.

Religious conversion in the real world is a complex tug-of-war between competing movements and secular forces played out over the fractal geometry of networks of social relations. Our first conversion simulation will simplify some of these factors mercilessly, thereby allowing us to focus on the constantly changing rate at which individuals are recruited to an irresistibly attractive religious movement. In the absence of any kind of social friction or other force counteracting the movement, recruitment happens so quickly it is hard to see what is happening. Therefore, we will incorporate one simple retardant, namely a relatively sparse social network.

We imagine that half of the houses of Cyburg have residents who are comfortably members of the same denomination, call them Unitarians. Thus, we start with 22,050 Unitarians and 22,050 vacant homes. We then add one evangelist for a different denomination, let us say a Mormon, who moves into a vacant home in the very center of town. (No aspersions on readers who happen to be members of the Unitarian-Universalists or Church of Jesus Christ of Latter-Day Saints; we simply want familiar denomination names that vary from simulation to simulation.) With luck, the Mormon will convert all the Unitarians to his church. The Catholic hero of the previous chapter was Andrew, so in alphabetical order we will call this Mormon missionary *Brigham*.

As in the simulations described in the previous chapter, on each turn the computer sequentially selects 44,100 homes at random (some by accident being selected two or more times, and others, skipped). But this time there are no conditions of satisfaction and no moving from one place to another. Instead, we have one very simple rule. When the computer selects a Unitarian, if the Unitarian has a Mormon near neighbor, then he immediately becomes a Mormon as well. Unitarians are not allowed to recruit Mormons, so this is a very one-sided game.

I ran this simulation once, continuing until all available Unitarians had been converted, which took fully 111 turns, saving full information about the town after each turn. At the end, 21,510 Unitarians had become Mormons, leaving 540 unconverted Unitarians who were socially isolated individuals or small groups and thus could not be reached through the extended social network that linked all the other residents of town. On the first turn, Brigham recruited 2 of his near neighbors who then recruited 3 of their own neighbors before the turn was over, yielding a total of 5 converts plus Brigham or 6 Mormons. In the second turn, 13 were converted by Brigham and his first followers, and in the third turn 9 were recruited. Naturally, the number recruited per turn bounces up and down at random, but the general trend over the first 40 or more turns was upward. On turn 21 the number of new recruits passed 100 for the first time, and the peak was on turn 66 when 467 Unitarians switched over to Mormonism. Then the growth slowed, dropping below 100 new recruits on turn 90, and finishing up with these numbers in the last 5 turns: 12, 6, 2, 4, and 3.

Figure 3.1 shows the rise and fall of recruitment visually, in what clearly looks like a normal curve overlaid by random jumps up and down. The rate of recruitment starts low, rises, then falls back to zero. More importantly, the rate of increase in recruitment grows (as the curve turns upward from the left-hand tail of the distribution), then shrinks (as the curve flattens out), and then becomes negative (as the curve falls), finally slowing its drop as it again approaches zero (the right-hand tail of the distribution).

When numbers of cases can be graphed by a normal curve, 64.26 percent of the cases are within one standard deviation of the mean. Another 13.59 percent are between one and two standard deviations below the mean, and 2.28 percent are more than two standard deviations below the mean. Here, the mean is turn 56.4, the average turn on which one of the 21,510 converts was gained. The

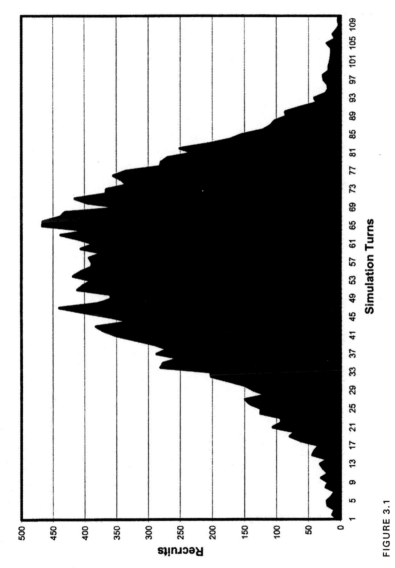

FIGURE 3.1

Recruits to a Religious Movement on Each of 111 Simulation Turns.

innovators would be the 2.28 percent or 490 who joined first, before the end of turn 19. But we know that that there is nothing special about these 490 people, except that they happened to live near the original Mormon and were reached by the expanding wave of Mormons early in the diffusion process. Thus, figure 3.1 shows that a normal curve can be the result of diffusion through the social structure of a community, in which individuals and their social locations vary only randomly.

A different insight can be obtained by graphing the growth of Mormons in Cyburg not in terms of how many new members are added in each turn, but how many members the movement has in total, from turn to turn. Figure 3.2 graphs the data this way, and the change in scale almost completely hides the random variations to show a very smooth sigmoid curve.

As the simulation runs, the number of movement members who are literally in a position to recruit new members changes. A brand-new member must have at least one Mormon neighbor, or he would not have joined, but the other neighbors may not already be Mormons. Thus, they are available for recruiting. But after all of a Mormon's neighbors have joined, there is no one left for that person to recruit. We could say that person has been smothered by fellow members and no longer has social ties to nonmembers who could be recruited. Thus, as the movement grows, it is not only true that new people are added who could recruit others, but also that old members are smothered so they can no longer recruit. As we will consider again in the following chapter, this is one of the reasons why religious movements often make a special effort to build social bonds with new people, rather than relying upon the existing social network for their recruiting efforts.

A third way of graphing the growth of a religious movement is in terms of how many new recruits join in a particular span of time, as a fraction of the number of existing members. Figure 3.3 shows that this measure drops very quickly at the beginning, before leveling out near zero. We do not actually graph what happens in the first step, in which 1 member (Brigham) recruits 5 in the first turn, because this would stretch the vertical scale of the graph so badly we could no longer see what is happening for most of the turns. On the second turn, 6 members recruit 13 more, which means 2.17 new members for each existing member. The next turn, only 0.47 new members join for each existing one, and by turn 28 this measure has dropped below 0.1, and on the very last turn it is 0.00014.

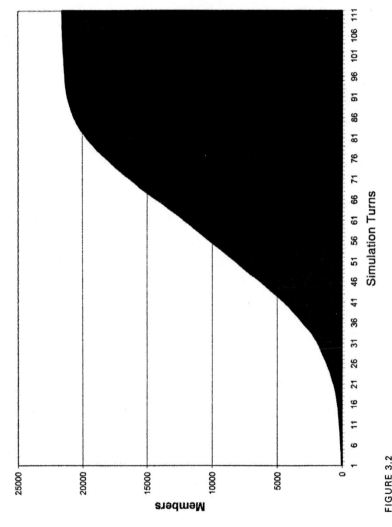

FIGURE 3.2
Total Size of a Religious Movement Recruiting Randomly.

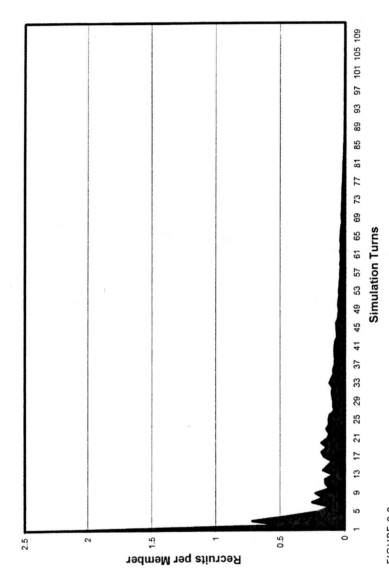

FIGURE 3.3
New Recruits as a Fraction of Existing Members.

As Stark and Lynne Roberts explained back in 1982, members of a religious movements may become discouraged if it is growing too slowly in their personal experience, even if it enjoys an objectively high annual growth rate. For example, in straightforward numerical simulations, they calculated that an annual growth rate of 20 percent would allow a group of 20 members to grow to 1.6 billion after a century (Stark and Roberts 1982, 349). Although this would be spectacular growth by historical standards, the individual member would have the satisfaction of recruiting just one other person every five years. In figure 3.3, we see that individual members would see their apparent recruiting effectiveness drop catastrophically after the first few turns, and this could indeed cause unwarranted disillusionment.

COMPETITIVE RECRUITMENT

It is very seldom that one religious movement completely dominates a religious market. More commonly, several different movements compete, and there are many factors that can promote or retard the growth of one against the growth of another (Stark 1996a, 1996b). Here we will take a small step forward by considering just the factor of membership size, when size is connected to the probability of conversion.

We need a theory of social influence that will tell us when an individual would tend to convert to a new religious affiliation. In the previous simulation, we assumed that one denomination was able to recruit with perfect efficiency, and now we need a more complex rule that allows each denomination to recruit from any of the others. The classic theoretical formulation of social influence theory is Sutherland's *Differential Association Theory*. This is a nine-step model that was originally applied to criminal behavior, but is theoretically appropriate for any kind of belief or behavior that could be the basis of a subculture, and religious movements and denominations are indeed subcultures. Others have offered their own variants; for example, Burgess and Akers (1966) reformulated differential association in terms of behavioral reinforcement. Here I will adapt to religion the nine steps as Sutherland stated them in 1947.

1. Religious behavior is learned.
2. In interaction with other persons in a process of communication.
3. Principally within intimate personal groups.

4. The learning includes
   a. religious practices, and
   b. religious beliefs, attitudes, and values.
5. The religious beliefs, attitudes, and values are learned from definitions favorable to acceptance of the particular religion or unfavorable.
6. A person converts to a religion because of an excess of definitions favorable to the religion over definitions unfavorable to the religion.
7. Differential associations may vary in frequency, duration, priority, and intensity.
8. The process of religious learning involves all the mechanisms that are involved in any other learning.
9. While religious behavior is an expression of general needs and values, it is not explained by those general needs and values, since nonreligious behavior is an expression of the same needs and values.

This model says a lot, too much to be considered at length now. It is primarily a cognitive theory. For Sutherland, the associations were mental associations, and therefore this conceptualization is very congenial for the kinds of artificial intelligence we will employ later on, which very specifically model the strength of associations between ideas in the mind. But the dynamic heart of the theory is the reception of communication messages from other people. While the model talks about an excess of definitions, it might just as well say an excess of definers, because people will receive more messages favorable to a religion if they come from a larger number of adherents of the religion. Thus, while we will return to definitions and mental associations later, for now we can operationalize differential association as most criminologists in fact did, as a theory about the characteristics of people with whom one associates.

I set the religious population of Cyburg at 44,100, with no vacant homes, such that 40 percent (16,640) of the people were Baptists. Another 30 percent (13,230) were Methodists, 20 percent (8,820) were Lutherans, and 10 percent (4,410) were Episcopalians. It is important to note that in the real world these denominations differ in terms of how vigorously they try to recruit new members, and in terms of how social class inspires people to switch to one or another of these denominations. But in this simulation, the only difference is the number of members.

With Differential Association Theory in mind, I imposed a decision rule that governed conversion based on the social influence of one's neighbors. That is, on a given turn the computer would tally the denominations of the people living around the given individual. If one denomination were more numerous than the others, the person would convert to that denomination. In this particular simulation, the computer did not take the individual's current denomination into account. Thus, people are not assumed to have any kind of internal, denominational loyalty or commitment, but are entirely influenced by the people they interact with socially.

The simulation ran to completion, reaching a configuration in which no further conversions could take place. At that point, the difference in size among denominations had increased significantly. Baptists had increased from 40.00 percent to 75.57 percent of the population, whereas the other groups had all declined. Methodists had dropped from 30.00 percent to 20.61 percent, Lutherans from 20.00 percent to 3.63 percent, and Episcopalians from 10.00 percent all the way down to 0.19 percent.

A granularity analysis is also striking. Fully 33,128 residents of the town were part of a huge, extended Baptist group. There were also five separate Baptist congregations with 18, 19, 27, 57, and 74 members. And the remaining 4 Baptists were socially isolated, lodged apart from any coreligionists along the boundaries between other denominations. There were 6 isolated Methodists plus fully 152 congregations of Methodists ranging from 10 to 379 members. There were 53 isolated Lutheran individuals plus 86 small Lutheran groups ranging from 3 to 82 members. Fully 36 of the 82 remaining Episcopalians were isolated individuals, and the 46 others were in 4 small groups of 4, 12, 14, and 16 members.

Of course, in a real town, these smaller groups would have in fact merged together into congregations whose members were geographically dispersed across the community. But this analysis of granularity reveals how devastating the success of a dominant religious movement can be on the social structure of opposing groups.

CONCENTRATION OF FORCES

My great-grandfather William Folwell Bainbridge was a scholar and an American Baptist minister who published three books based on a two-year, globe-circling research expedition he carried out in 1879 and 1880. The first two books, *Round the World Tour of Christian Missions* (1882) and *Along the Lines at the Front* (1882), were explicitly intended to establish a science of missions, whereas the third, a novel called *Self Giving* (1883) that satirized many real missionaries, did not exactly endear him to his colleagues. I introduce my great-grandfather here not out of nepotism, but because he offered a theoretical insight that will be useful to us.

In *Along the Lines at the Front*, William Folwell Bainbridge employed military metaphors to analyze the campaign to Christianize the world. After spending many weeks in Burma, he concluded that American Baptists should send many more missionaries there, even though there already were quite a few: "Without thoroughly understanding the situation, it may seem strange that ninety-four missionaries—nearly all of them confined in their work to the lower half of the country—should not be deemed an adequate supply. Already it would appear that Burmah is three times as strongly occupied in proportion as India. But in every great warfare there are points of concentration. More soldiers were massed against Richmond than against Port Hudson or Atlanta" (Bainbridge 1882a, 164–65). He had observed the Union Army in action against Lee when he was a student minister, and extensive reading had taught him much about military strategy and tactics. Thus, he understood well the principle of *concentration of forces.*

A numerically inferior army can triumph if it maneuvers itself into local supremacy over part of the opposing force. The same can be true for religious movements. A concentrated minority can function locally as a majority. If it deploys that local majority effectively, it can ultimately outgrow minority status. In military science, the concentration of forces is amenable to mathematical analysis (Lanchester 1956). Here, we will employ computer simulation to explore concentration from the standpoint of the social science of religion.

I compared two runs in an experiment that set them up similarly, except that the denomination of interest was socially concentrated in one and dispersed in the other. At the start of each, Cyburg had 10 religious denominations. Nine of them were of equal size, each having 4,851 members, which is exactly 11 percent of the population. The remaining denomination had only 441 members, just one percent of the population. They will be the denomination of interest, and we can call them Jehovah's Witnesses. The decision rule will be set the same as in the previous simulation: People will convert to the plurality denomination among their neighbors.

In one of the two experimental conditions, the 441 members of Jehovah's Witnesses are dispersed at random throughout the town. Like the smallest denomination in the previous simulation, we would have to predict that it will lose members catastrophically. Indeed, its membership plummeted from 441 to only 30, from 1 percent to 0.07 percent of the town. The other 9 denominations gained or lost slightly, in the random tug-of-war between them, and wound up ranging from 9.68 percent to 11.81 percent.

In the other experimental condition, the 441 Witnesses were concentrated in a 21-by-21 square, right in the center of town. They were still outnumbered town-wide, but having concentrated they could defend themselves better. Indeed, because the other 9 denominations were dispersed rather than concentrated, we would predict that the Witnesses would grow because of their concentration. This is exactly what happened. Starting from a concentration in the center of town, the Witnesses grew from 441 to 592 members before their growth stalled. In percentage terms, this was an increase from 1 percent to 1.34 percent. At the end, other denominations ranged from 10.35 to 11.40 percent.

Again, it was worth looking at the granularity of the results of this experiment. In the dispersed version, at the end, one concentrated group of 15 Witnesses had emerged out of the random chaos, and an equal number of individual Witnesses were able to survive along the boundaries between other groups. In the concentrated version, all 592 Witnesses were indeed positioned as one large bloc at the center of town. Further expansion had been blocked by a ring of smaller groups of members of other denominations, and by a few lone individuals at the intersections between other groups.

Given that all the denominations were initially small, and the 9 that boasted 11 percent of the population each were randomly dispersed around town, it is worth noting that organization arose out of the chaos in both versions of the experiment. In the version where Witnesses were dispersed, 34 congregations of the other denominations wound up with at least 100 members, the largest having 267. Except for the fate of the Witnesses, the results of the version in which they had been concentrated were almost identical. The other 9 denominations wound up with 32 congregations having over 100 members, the largest of which had 261.

CHAOS AND COMPLEXITY

To explore the slow turning of the wheel of random fate, Cyburg's population was set so that there were 10 equal denominations, each with 4,410 members, or 10 percent of the total. A new conversion decision rule was employed. On a given person's turn, the computer would select one of the person's neighbors at random, and if that neighbor was a different denomination, convert the person to it. This models, if you will, the random influence of one very close friend. Like the rule that converts a person to the plurality denomination among neighbors, this rule would give an advantage to any denomination whose members were more numerous than the average. However, we start out with exactly equal numbers across the city as a whole, so there is no initial advantage.

In any local region, by pure chance, one denomination may have more members, and therefore be in a position to grow even larger. This is one of Boudon's *magnification* processes, mentioned in the previous chapter. A size advantage tends to be self-reinforcing. Furthermore, in this simulation there is nothing to halt the growth of a denomination, unless it is a string of bad luck, because unlike the case under the plurality rule, concentration of one denomination in a local bloc does not prevent another denomination from invading that area.

However, we are all familiar with the law of large numbers, mentioned in the last chapter in connection with convergent phenomena. On average, things average out. Over the very long run, random drift can produce changes even in a large population, but the run may be very long indeed. This has been one of the challenges for theorists of biological evolution who focus on population biology, and it is one of the reasons they suggest that evolution may occur more rapidly in small subpopulations that are somewhat isolated from the rest of the species (Mayr 1964). Indeed, the simulation described here did not reach completion for nearly 2,000 turns, much more than the 50 turns often required for the other simulations of this chapter and the previous one.

Table 3.1 gives the denominational census of Cyburg, every 200 turns, and it shows that random processes can produce size differences between denominations. All 10 denominations begin with exactly 10 percent of the 44,100 residents of Cyburg. But after 200 turns—200 times 44,100 decisions about converting—their sizes ranged from 7.35 percent to 13.45 percent. Six of the denominations grow at the expense of the other four. Note that Denomination 3 has taken a big lead, 13.45 percent compared with 11.88 percent for

Table 3.1. Random Triumph of One Denomination over Others by Recruitment

Denomination	At Start (%)	Turn 200 (%)	Turn 400 (%)	Turn 600 (%)	Turn 800 (%)	Turn 1,000 (%)	Turn 1,200 (%)	Turn 1,400 (%)	Turn 1,600 (%)	Turn 1,800 (%)
1	10	8.07	6.24	6.63	6.91	3.37	2.07	0.55	0.00	0.00
2	10	7.39	7.48	4.43	1.54	1.03	0.51	0.00	0.00	0.00
3	10	13.45	15.79	10.19	6.35	5.04	4.61	2.70	0.23	0.00
4	10	7.83	7.25	6.79	2.57	0.76	0.00	0.00	0.00	0.00
5	10	7.35	6.10	5.46	4.89	3.11	3.01	0.77	0.00	0.00
6	10	10.33	7.49	6.73	10.53	9.58	5.06	1.39	0.55	0.00
7	10	10.85	6.56	5.68	3.41	3.46	1.04	0.02	0.00	0.00
8	10	11.88	10.58	12.63	8.00	2.83	0.82	0.12	0.00	0.00
9	10	11.70	19.01	28.22	39.84	54.03	69.83	85.56	94.08	99.73
10	10	11.16	13.51	13.24	15.96	16.80	13.05	8.90	5.14	0.27

Denomination 8. Luck has given Denomination 3 an early lead, and one might want to predict that it will soon vanquish the nine other denominations.

Indeed, by turn 400, Denomination 3 has grown to 15.79 percent of the total, and now six denominations have fallen well below 10 percent, the lowest at only 6.10 percent. However, Denomination 3 is no longer the largest, because Denomination 9 had surged to 19.01 percent. This illustrates the fact that statistical advantages can be fleeting, especially at medium levels of intensity. It is true that the simulation was set in such a way that large denominations were more able to recruit than smaller denominations. But the 1.75 percentage-point advantage that Denomination 3 had over Denomination 9 was not yet decisive, and there was a moderate probability that this advantage could be overcome by random processes.

By turn 600, the picture has sharpened considerably. Now, Denomination 9 holds a huge advantage, 28.22 percent or more than twice the size of the second-place denomination, which is now Denomination 10 at 13.24 percent. Denomination 3 has dropped back near its original starting size, and poor Denomination 2 has dropped below half that to 4.43 percent. Mathematical analysis could tell us the probability that Denomination 9's growth could be halted at this point, but it seems to have a solid advantage that should translate into further growth.

Looking across the table, we see that Denomination 9's march to supremacy continues unchallenged. By 1,200 turns, one of the other denominations has dropped to zero membership. In a simulation such as this, once a denomination is extinct, nothing can resurrect it. As more and more denominations die out, the dominance of Denomination 9 become unassailable. On turn 1,800, only one other denomination still exists, Denomination 10 with 0.27 percent, and before turn 2,000 it also succumbs.

This simulation has been run several times, and on different occasions different denominations win out. This really is a random process that in every case eventually grinds through until only one denomination reigns supreme. It is not possible to predict which denomination that will be, short of actually running the simulation through to completion. To say that it is random is not to suggest there is free will anywhere inside my computer.

The programming language I used incorporates a pseudorandom-number-generating routine that starts with a number and then performs a mathematical transformation to create a new number. The same transformation is done again to create a third number, and then a fourth, and so on. For example, the transformation could be to divide the first number by a large prime number and take the remainder as the next number. The programming language provides two options for setting the original number: RandSeed (when I would input the number I wanted to start with) or Randomize (in which the computer takes its starting number from the clock: how many seconds there have been since midnight). If I run the simulation twice, using the same RandSeed, the results will work out exactly the same, to the finest detail. But I still could not predict those results without running the simulation once.

This is an adequate operational definition of *deterministic chaos*, a branch of mathematics that looks at *nonlinear recursive functions*: repeating algorithms (like dividing and taking the remainder) that cannot be reduced to a simpler formula (for example, by calculus) that would predict the result a specified number of steps forward. Chaos theory became fashionable in the 1980s in general scientific and philosophical circles (Mandelbrot 1983; Hao 1984; Gleick 1987; Goerner 1994), and it does a very good job of modeling well-defined complex systems, such as the dynamic evolution of the orbits of planets in a solar system. In the 1990s the idea of deterministic chaos entered sociology, notably in computer simulation studies of social network dynamics by Barry Markovsky (1992) and of international arms races by Robert Leik and Barbara Meeker (1995), and a special session of the annual meeting of the American Sociological Association (Eve, Horsfall, and Lee 1997; Bainbridge 1997b).

SUMMATION

Human religious history was powerfully shaped by a fundamentally random event that occurred in Babylon on June 13, 323 B.C. At the tender age of 32, Alexander the Great, conqueror of vast territories and myriad peoples, died of fever. According to legend, as he was dying his generals stood around him and asked him to appoint a successor. Instead, he supposedly tossed his ring of authority into the air and said, "To the strongest!" In any case, on that day the Greek conquests ceased, and his realm broke into three lesser parts. Had Alexander lived another 30 years, he would have consolidated the Greek empire and possibly expanded it to the west, as he had already done to the east. In any case, Rome would have lost the Macedonian wars a century later (which it actually won because it was facing only the smallest fragment of Alexander's empire), and there would have been no Roman Empire. Without Rome, the history of Western Europe would have been incalculably different; we presumably would not be using the Roman alphabet today, and it is even possible to argue that the winner in the contest among messianic religions two millennia ago would not have been Christianity but Mithraism or something else. Remember that Jesus was born in Bethlehem, rather than elsewhere under very different conditions, specifically because Caesar Augustus required all the world to be taxed.

Gaius Julius Caesar, uncle of Augustus, showed a fine appreciation of the nature of chaotic events in the words he spoke when he led his army across the Rubicon river into Italy, thereby defying the Republic: The die is cast. (*Alea jacta est*, and our technical term *aleatoric* refers to chance processes.) At certain historical moments, social organizations concentrate power in a person or a decision such that very slight changes could take history down a very different path: the premature death from illness of Alexander the Great, Hitler's decision to invade the Soviet Union before Britain had been defeated, Pickett's charge at the Battle of Gettysburg, which may have sealed the fate of the Confederacy. Without Caesar, there might have been subsequent Russian and German empires, but they would not have called their leaders *caesars* (czars and kaisers). Alexander's death, Caesar's decision, and their consequences are prime examples of divergent phenomena in human history.

This chapter has reminded us of some classic sociological theory relevant to religious conversion, and then explored one of the central themes of that theory: social influence. Other themes introduced here will be examined closely in later chapters. Our model of social influence was extremely simple, involving no real intelligence on the part of the simulated people. Thus, substantial machine intelligence is also reserved for later chapters. Indeed, the aim of this chapter was to prepare the way for complexity and intelligence by establishing baselines of phenomena in which behavior does not depend upon these qualities.

We saw that an extremely simple model of recruitment to a growing social movement can produce the normal curve of recruitment rates that is often taken as evidence that some people in the population are by nature innovators or early adopters. Of course, people very well may differ in their propensity to join a new movement, but the first simulation described in this chapter shows one should be cautious about leaping to this assumption. The dynamic geometry of diffusion alone can explain much about the shape of movement growth. Rates of growth that can lead to rapid expansion of a movement may, nonetheless, seem very slow to individual members, and those who have already recruited their neighbors in the social network may no longer be in a position to help the group grow further.

Most religious conversion takes place in an environment where multiple denominations or movements compete. In the absence of other factors, larger groups have an advantage in recruitment driven by social influence. Concentration of forces can allow a minority group to behave like a majority locally, both to resist being overwhelmed by a larger group, and even to recruit from larger groups so long as the latter are not themselves concentrated.

4

Fellowship

Although chapter 3 talked about recruitment across a social network, it offered an extremely limited notion of what a network is. For one thing, it assumed that near neighbors socially influence each other, whereas in the real world they may ignore each other, depending upon whether a positive relationship exists between them. For another, the previous chapter assumed that social networks are static structures, whereas real networks are dynamic, forming and reforming as relationships are born and die. The simulations described in this chapter will give the social network of Cyburg complex, dynamic structures. To make sense of them, we need analytical tools, such as triad analysis and Fritz Heider's Balance Theory.

ANALYSIS OF NETWORK STRUCTURE

The metaphor *social network* has become commonplace. Everybody can imagine a network as a diagram of lines (representing social bonds) connecting squares (representing individual people), even if they are unaware of the fact that such diagrams are called *sociograms* and were developed by Jacob Moreno in the 1930s. Moreno was a remarkable character with many of the qualities of a cult founder, who late in his life professed to be receiving messages directly from God. He was the inventor of psychodrama and apparently wanted to surpass Sigmund Freud within the field of psychotherapy. Like many intellectuals who were appalled by World War I, he believed that a new science was needed to prevent future such catastrophes. He called his candidate *sociometry*, the study of social relationships. He introduced this science in a strange yet sociologically rigorous book titled *Who Shall Survive?* Moreno is practically forgotten today, but sociometry, narrowly defined as the study of social networks, is an established field of sociology, and the journal he founded is still published under a different name.

Perhaps the simplest measure for describing a network is its density, the fraction of the possible social bonds that actually exist. For example, among three people there can be as few as zero social bonds, and as many as three social bonds. (With Alice, Bill, and Connie, the possible relationships are Alice-Bill, Alice-Connie, and Bill-Connie.) The formula for calculating the number of possible bonds (reciprocal relationships or pairs of people) in a population of N people is $N(N-1)/2$. In a town of 44,100 people, the possible number of bonds, therefore, is 972,405,000. For sake of simplicity, the simulations described in this chapter limit social relationships to near neighbors. (Later chapters will abandon that limitation.) Each person has eight near neighbors, except those at the edge of town who have fewer, and thus the total possible number of social bonds in Cyburg is a more tractable 175,142. If, at a particular point in a simulation run, there were actually only 87,571 bonds, then the network density would be $87,571/175,142 = 0.5$ or 50 percent.

Density is an important measure, but it does not tell the whole story. Figures 4.1A and 4.1B show two social networks, each having 25 people and 36 social bonds. The maximum number of possible bonds between near neighbors in squares with five people on a side is 72, so the densities of the two networks are both $36/72 = 0.5 = 50$ percent. But the networks look very different. In one, the bonds are distributed at random, whereas in the other they are clumped in

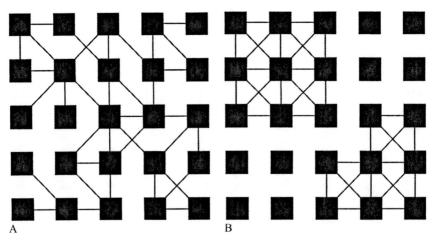

A   B

FIGURE 4.1A–B
(A) An Open Social Network; (B) A Closed Social Network.

Table 4.1. Census of Triads in Two Social Networks

Bonds in Triad	Open Network	Closed Network
0-bond Triads	7	21
1-bond Triads	23	14
2-bond Triads	27	1
3-bond Triads	7	28
Total	64	64

subgroups or cliques. These can be described, respectively, as open and closed social networks. Clearly, we need a measure of the closure of a social network. An effective but simple approach is to focus on *triads*, relationships involving not two but three people, and count the number of social bonds in each triad (Johnson and McCann 1982; Skvoretz, Fararo, and Agneessens 2004).

Each of the two networks contains 64 different triads, given the near-neighbor limitation. Table 4.1 reports censuses of the triads in both, and the results show an extreme contrast. In the open network, triads with 0 bonds and 3 bonds are both rare, whereas triads with 1 or 2 bonds are common. The opposite is true for the closed network, where 0-bond and 3-bond triads predominate. The biggest contrast concerns 2-bond triads—trios of people that contain two social relationships but the third is missing. (Alice is friends with Bill and with Connie, but Bill and Connie are not friends with each other.) Indeed, the fraction of triads with 2 bonds can be taken as a simple but fairly valid measure of the openness of a network. Here, the percentages are 42.2 versus 1.6.

Analysis in terms of triads is not only methodologically sound and computationally convenient but also has a solid connection to theory. Specifically, triads are fundamental to the Balance Theory that was proposed by Heider (1958; cf. Homans 1974). Heider's paradigm focuses on two people who share a relationship, and their attitudes toward an object. I am using the term *object* here in the psychological sense, to refer to anything about which the two people can have thoughts and feelings, including a religious practice, a belief, or even a third person.

Suppose Hathor and Christian are friends, and Christian has become involved with a radical religious group that is just beginning to recruit converts. In fact, this is a real example, and the group was the Process Church of the Final Judgement, about which I wrote a book based on ethnographic observations and interviews (Bainbridge 1978, 1992a). Hathor and Christian share a positive relationship, and Christian has developed a positive relationship with the Process, but Hathor lacks a relationship to the Process. This is an unstable situation. The Process is demanding so much time and emotional investment from Christian that it has implications for his relationship with Hathor. The situation can become stabilized if either Hathor joins the Process as well or if Christian and Hathor break off their relationship. That is, a 2-bond triad is unstable and tends to morph into either a 3-bond triad or a 1-bond triad.

Needless to say, real social networks in fact contain a good deal of instability. The more salient the relationships are to the people involved, the more pressure they will feel to adjust their relationships to bring them into better balance. Part of the pressure is social; Christian will invite Hathor to accompany him to the Process and take part in its activities. But part of it also is purely cognitive. Hathor values Christian, which makes his judgment salient for her. People get much of their information from other people, including explanations about how to lead a satisfying life and testimonials that encourage religious conversion (Stark and Bainbridge 1987). If Hathor rejects Christian's advice that the Process is worth her involvement, she thereby rejects a part of him.

Put in terms of cognition, it is inconsistent for Hathor to be very close to Christian yet think significantly differently than he does. People who interact frequently will tend to become more alike, and thus continuing to think differently will be a source of tension (Homans 1950). The classic theory of cognitive consistency, Leon Festinger's *cognitive dissonance theory*, was first illustrated through a field study of a cult (Festinger, Riecken, and Schachter 1956; Festinger 1957), so there is good reason to apply it to religion. Heider's Balance Theory can be seen as the classic adaptation of cognitive dissonance to social relationships, thus importing concepts from cognitive psychology to social psychology. In the given event, Hathor did join the Process, and the unbalanced 2-bond triad became a balanced 3-bond triad.

BALANCE IN CYBURG

Whereas in the previous chapter the social network was stable, and people converted from one denomination to another, this section will explore a dynamic network with stable denominational affiliation. After we become familiar with some features of changing network structure, we will look at situations in which both affiliation and the network are dynamic.

The simulations in this chapter imagine that Cyburg has between two and ten denominations, depending upon the goals of the particular simulation, with approximately equal memberships. At the beginning of a simulation, the user selects how many denominations there should be. The software then goes through the list of 44,100 people and assigns denominations to them on the basis of probabilities and random numbers. That is, if the user has decided there should be seven denominations, each simulated person will have a one-seventh chance of being assigned to any particular one of them. At the end of the assignment process, each denomination will have approximately one-seventh of the total population, or about 6,300 members—but not exactly. Here, for example, are the actual sizes of seven denominations at the beginning of such a run: 6,365, 6,316, 6,244, 6,346, 6,298, 6,184, and 6,344.

Our first run will have just two denominations, hold the denominational memberships constant, and see what happens if the simulated people follow Balance Theory concerning denominational membership. If two neighbors have a social bond, but they are of different denominations, they will break that bond. If two neighbors lack a bond but are of the same denomination, they will develop a bond. The way the computer accomplishes this is to select a person at random and scan through his eight possible social relationships, adding a bond if necessary to every neighbor of the same denomination, and breaking a bond to every neighbor of a different denomination.

At the beginning of the simulation, the density of social bonds was set (again using random numbers and probabilities) to be approximately 50 percent, and turned out to be 50.11 percent. As desired, the two denominations are approximately equal in size, having 21,935 and 22,162 members. During the run, as we specified, nobody converts from one denomination to another, but about half of the social bonds are broken, and about half of the social bonds that exist at the end were created during the run. After all this activity, the social bond density is 50.05 percent, almost exactly what it was at the beginning, despite the huge volatility of social relationships. This results from the fact that with two denominations of approximately equal size, lost bonds and gained bonds will nearly cancel out.

What will all this activity do to the local closure of the network? We can answer this by examining triad censuses representing the beginning and end of the simulation, and in so doing we will illustrate through a simple example how computer simulation may facilitate logical deduction of theoretical propositions.

The simulated people acted upon Balance Theory based on their religious traits. Their behavior was not in any way caused by their attitudes toward the social-bond triads of which they are parts. (Alice did not care whether Bill and Connie are friends, but adjusted her own bonds to each of them in accordance with their religious affiliations.) With that in mind, consider this theoretical proposition: "A triad balanced for traits will automatically also be balanced for bonds." If this is true, then during the simulation run 2-bond triads will vanish, even though the agents were not paying attention to whether there was a third bond between the two agents they were connected to.

Table 4.2 gives the triad censuses before and after the run, and it confirms the theoretical proposition. The number of 2-bond triads drops from 65,390 to 0, or from 37.42 percent to 0 percent. By the simple laws of probability, at the beginning of the simulation, when bonds are assigned at random to 50 percent of the pairs, we would expect one-eighth of the triads to have 0 bonds, and another one-eighth to have 3 bonds. We would expect three-eighths to have 1 bond, and the remaining three-eighths to have 2 bonds. Since one-eighth is 12.50 percent, and three-eighths is 37.50 percent, that is indeed what we see at the beginning, within a very small random error. The complete extinction of 2-bond triads would be exceedingly improbable purely by chance, and nicely demonstrates that *a triad balanced for traits will automatically also be balanced for bonds.*

The simulation illustrates the ambivalent effect of religious particularism upon social relations in a society. In this particular simulation, the density of social relations does not change significantly, so it would be wrong to say that religious intolerance had caused social disorganization and anomie. However, the triad census becomes almost entirely 1-bond triads (which tend to

Table 4.2. **Census of Triads before and after Trait Balancing Run**

Bonds in Triad	Triads Before	Triads After	Percent Before (%)	Percent After (%)
0-bond Triads	21,694	6	12.42	0.00
1-bond Triads	65,579	130,970	37.53	74.96
2-bond Triads	65,390	0	37.42	0.00
3-bond Triads	22,061	43,748	12.63	25.04
Total	174,724	174,724	100.00	100.00

mark boundaries between local congregations of the two denominations) and 3-bond triads (high-solidarity social cores of local congregations.) The two denominations have segregated from each other, while increasing their internal solidarity to the extent that the distributions of affiliations in each neighborhood permitted them to do so. Figure 4.2 depicts the texture of the resulting social network.

This figure shows exactly 1 percent of the entire town, as it was at the end of this simulation, containing 441 people. Each square represents one agent,

FIGURE 4.2
Two Denominations, after Affiliations and Bonds Were Balanced.

colored either black or white to represent the two denominations. Each line is a social bond, and the stubs around the edges represent bonds to agents who are not shown. Wherever chance has placed members of the same denomination together in a neighborhood, we see a dense tracing of bonds. Wherever chance has produced pluralism, we see a low density of bonds. At places, long fingers of one denomination reach into an area dominated by the other. In the real world, such regions of the social world are especially fertile ground for conversions to or from a given denomination.

RELIGIOUS PLURALISM

Our next simulations will combine Heider's Balance Theory with Sutherland's Differential Association Theory, keeping our focus primarily on the consequences for the structure of social networks, and we will do so while exploring an interesting facet of one of the unresolved debates in the sociology of religion.

In the early 1990s, social scientists began debating the relationship between religious pluralism and commitment (Warner 1993). Finke and Stark (1988, 1989a, 1989b, 1992; Finke 1989; Stark and Finke 2000) described religion as a market economy in which denominations compete with each other for members as corporations compete for customers (cf. Jelen 2002). Different individuals and groups in society have different needs, cultures, and nonreligious affiliations, so therefore religious pluralism should increase commitment by offering each person the style of religion that suits him or her best. In their empirical work, Finke and Stark have tried to show that rates of church membership are higher where there are more denominations in the religious marketplace.

Other researchers argued that religious pluralism has a negative effect on church membership (Breault 1989a, 1989b; Land, Deane, and Blau 1991; Blau, Land, and Redding 1992; Blau, Redding, and Land 1993; cf. Christiano 1987). Religious monopoly might be associated with higher rates of religious involvement, if individual affiliations are chiefly the result of social influence, and if social influence is most effective when it is monolithic. This perspective is identical with Differential Association Theory, and will be the focus of our explorations in this section.

Thus, the narrow debate over denominational diversity and religious mobilization bears directly upon two distinctive general models of group process. The diversity-mobilization argument conceptualizes group affiliation in terms of individual choices among competing suppliers, with individuals maximizing their satisfaction by selecting the suppliers that best meet their personal needs. The monopoly-mobilization argument sees affiliation in terms of the net power of social influences operating within a diffuse social network, wherein persons are more strongly impelled to join a group the greater the proportion of their consociates who are members.

In the vigorous debate over proper methods of empirical research that has raged in the journals over this issue, the theoretical underpinnings have tended to become obscured. It is widely assumed that the diversity-mobilization hypothesis is rooted in the Stark-Bainbridge theory of religion (Stark and Bainbridge 1985, 1987; cf. Finke and Stark 1988, 2000), which laid the ground-work for a market analysis of religion and sought to establish the sociology of religion on a more rigorous footing (Simpson 1990; Collins 1993). However, in truth the monopoly-mobilization hypothesis also can be derived from the Stark-Bainbridge theory. Indeed, I have taken the position (Bainbridge 1995a, 1995b) that both hypotheses are valid and merely describe counteracting forces. Which of the two forces will predominate depends upon the circumstances. In some cases the two forces may even act in consort. Perhaps the best ex-ample is Protestantism, a single tradition (thus taking advantage of a cultural monopoly) divided into denominations and sects that serve different slices of the market (thus taking advantage of diversity to mobilize diverse customers).

The simulation described here does not give the agents diverse needs, al-though the simulations described in the two concluding chapters do. Therefore, here we will not be testing the competing logics of the diversity-mobilization and monopoly-mobilization perspectives, but looking at some social-network consequences of religious pluralism that are relevant for theories incorporat-ing the monopoly-mobilization concept. An entire book could be devoted to this theme, so our brief exploration will be only a sample of what computer simulation can contribute to the debate.

We will examine the impact on the social network of different numbers of denominations—from 2 to 10—when Balance Theory is in operation either with or without differential association. As in the previous simulation, the memberships of the denominations will be approximately equal, and the social network will start out with a density of approximately 50 percent. In each case, we run the simulation until there are no more 2-bond triads, a practical indicator of the point after which no more significant changes would occur. In the first series of runs, only Balance Theory will be in effect. Table 4.3 gives the

Table 4.3. Effects of Religious Pluralism and Balance versus Differential Association

	Density of Social Network			Social Isolates in Population		
Number of Denominations	100% Balance Theory (%)	50% Balance Theory (%)	20% Balance Theory (%)	100% Balance Theory (%)	50% Balance Theory (%)	20% Balance Theory (%)
2	50.01	56.72	65.44	0.48	0.52	0.39
3	33.57	41.33	51.99	3.95	3.14	1.82
4	24.91	33.98	44.97	10.33	7.12	4.05
5	19.90	29.07	40.07	17.37	11.21	5.97
6	16.65	25.88	37.02	23.73	14.91	8.26
7	14.30	23.41	34.43	29.30	18.63	10.26
8	12.46	21.04	32.72	34.83	22.10	12.15
9	11.16	19.55	30.83	39.12	25.35	14.03
10	10.16	18.34	29.54	43.00	28.02	15.95

results of 27 simulation runs, 9 each under three different mixtures of balance and differential association.

Two columns of table 4.3, those labeled "100% Balance Theory," show the conclusions of runs in which differential association was switched off, so nobody converted from one denomination to another. As one might predict, the greater the number of denominations, the lower the resultant density of the social network. The more denominations there are, the fewer neighbors of any individual are likely to be of that person's own denomination and thus suitable for a social bond under Balance Theory. Thus, in the absence of any other factors, it is practically tautological that people who are willing to have relationships only with people of the same denomination are destined to have fewer relationships the more denominations there are.

The religious pluralism debate largely focused on mobilization, the fraction of the population that belongs to and participates in the activities of a religious group. In the context of our simple simulation, we can reasonably define mobilization as the fraction of the population with bonds to members of the same denomination. The converse of this, what might be called the unchurched, is the fraction who are social isolates, people who lack any social bonds—since in this simulation enduring bonds can be only to members of one's own faith. When the simulations start, with a network density of about 50 percent, social isolates tend to represent only about one-half of 1 percent of the population. But after running the computer program to its conclusion, with 10 denominations and no opportunity for conversion, social isolates increase to fully 43 percent.

This is a clear sign that religious pluralism can undercut mobilization, under some conditions. It is vital to remember, however, that we have excluded the market factors that proponents of the diversity-mobilization theory propose, so their theory is really not allowed to compete in these particular simulations. We have also excluded religious conversion, and it is time to reintroduce this important factor.

In the columns of table 4.3 labeled "50% Balance Theory," when each agent gets a turn to act, at random, half the time the person will follow Balance Theory, and the other half the time the agent will follow Differential Association Theory. It is as if the person flipped a coin. If it comes up heads, the agent will develop a bond with any neighbor of the same denomination, and break off any bonds with neighbors belonging to other denominations. If the coin comes up tails, the agent will scan the neighborhood, and if there is a majority denomination locally, the agent will convert to it.

It is worth noting that this book is oriented toward artificial intelligence simulations, and that as we progress through the chapters the intelligence of the agents will rise from near zero to something capable of significantly complex learning. To this point, we have chiefly told the agents what to think, so they have not needed minds of their own. Their intelligence has been primarily on the level of the community: artificial *social* intelligence. Complex social behaviors have arisen emergently from the interactions of very stupid individuals. Previously, individual agents have followed preprogrammed decision rules. Now, the very first glimmerings of autonomous decision making emerge in the probabilistic nature of choosing one of two theories to follow. Social scientists often model behavior statistically, so there is nothing unusual in letting probabilities decide how the agents will act. As with the mouse seeking cheese in a T-maze, introduced in chapter 1, a probabilistic decision process can be the basis on which we can later build much more complex learning and conceptualization into the agents.

Reintroducing religious conversion, by letting an agent follow Differential Association Theory about half the time, has a profound effect. Whether with 2 denominations or 10, the resultant social density is always higher, and the fraction of the population who are social isolates (i.e., the unchurched) is lower. Clearly, religious conversion mitigates the corrosive effect of religious pluralism on social networks. True, there is still a marked effect of increasing the number of denominations, but it is significantly muted.

The remaining two columns of table 4.3 report simulations in which agents follow Balance Theory only 20 percent of the time, and Differential Association Theory 80 percent of the time. The nine runs under this condition still result in a complete loss of 2-bond triads, but religious conversion is able to operate more strongly to incorporate individuals into a network of same-denomination other individuals, which we can conceptualize as congregations.

To get a sense of what Cyburg looks like at the end of a typical run in this series, figure 4.3 shows 1 percent of the town at the conclusion of a simulation with 5 denominations and in which Balance Theory operated 50 percent of the

FIGURE 4.3
Results of Combining Balance Theory with Differential Association Theory.

time. It is possible to spot a few social isolates—represented by squares that lack any social bonds—but most agents are linked into small groups, some of which are big enough to resemble congregations in the real world. Within themselves, these congregations have a high degree of social connection, although by the rules of this particular game they are disconnected from each other. Thus, the situation is strictly not one of social disorganization and anomie. Rather, social disorganization on the large scale of the entire town is offset by a high degree of local social organization. The experience of most individuals would not be one of anomie or alienation, but of social cohesion.

Thus, merely introducing the possibility of religious conversion significantly mitigates the negative effect of religious pluralism on mobilization. Presumably, adding market factors could have a further effect in the same direction. However, we are not done with network and conversion effects yet. In particular, we need to introduce the possibility that members of some religious groups might intentionally develop social bonds with people who are not already members, and thereby convert them to membership.

OUTREACH

Successful religious groups engage in a variety of methods for recruiting new members, and many sects are positively aggressive in accosting victims on the street and knocking on the doors of strangers' homes. The two high-tension religious movements I wrote book-length studies about, The Process and The Family (Children of God), both invested considerable time and effort meeting strangers in public places and either selling magazines or distributing free tracts (Bainbridge 1978, 2002). Processeans called their activity *donating*, and members of the Family called theirs *litnessing*, but in both cases the work served several functions. First of all, it was one of the important ways these groups collected money, because full-time members of both were discouraged from holding conventional jobs. Second, it kept members busy, with the benefits of physical exercise and outside social activity. But third, it was also certainly intended as a recruiting technique.

Outreach based on fleeting contacts with strangers does not work well at all. In an early article titled "Networks of Faith," Stark and I argued that development of interpersonal bonds is fundamental to successful recruitment to cults and sects, and that its power comes through gradual development of strong social ties with a few individuals, not through vast numbers of brief encounters (Stark and Bainbridge 1980a). In the previous chapter we quoted the Lofland-Stark model as saying a crucial step in religious conversion is when "an affective bond is formed . . . with one or more converts" or current members of the group. We also argued that Sutherland's differential association theory could be interpreted to mean that a person would be more likely to join under the influence of multiple members, although Sutherland himself used the term *association* to refer to mental connections rather than social bonds.

The simulations described in the previous section already made this point implicitly. Setting the computer program so that balance theory is in effect only 20 percent of the time, rather than 50 percent, has the effect of increasing the average duration of social bonds between agents who belong to different denominations, thereby increasing the chance that one of them will be converted. Now we will examine a similar set of experiments in which we add a very simple form of outreach.

Outreach is inserted in the part of the program that deals with balance theory. The user sets the probability of outreach, and then a random number decides whether outreach will happen in the particular turn. The outreach procedure itself is very simple. The agent develops a social bond with each of the near neighbors, regardless of what denomination each of them belongs to. This comes after balancing bonds, so the agent cannot break off any bonds to members of other denominations until the next time this agent balances bonds, although the other agents might break the bonds on their turns.

It is important to think social-structurally about outreach. The program allows us to set the outreach probability separately for each denomination, but not for each individual member. Thus, if a particular denomination engages in outreach, two or more members may engage in outreach to the same nonmember, thereby putting the nonmember in a position where differential association may cause the nonmember to convert. In addition, this particular program does not allow us to distinguish denominations in terms of how attractive their beliefs and practices may be to certain nonmembers. Here, conversion is entirely a matter of some bonds and social influence. Other factors may also be important in the real world, but by restricting this set of simulations to social influence we can explore its distinctive significance.

Outreach is a double-edged sword. If an agent belongs to a particular group, say the Process, but is not connected by many bonds to fellow Processeans, the agent is vulnerable to being recruited away. Suppose Hathor is a Processean with only one bond to another Processean, and she engages in outreach, building

Table 4.4. Membership Growth of a Denomination Practicing Outreach

Number of Denominations	Members at Start	Members after 1 Turn	Members after 10 Turns	Members after 100 Turns
2	22,043	22,279	21,650	18,326
3	14,670	15,001	15,910	16,111
4	11,031	11,385	13,931	17,832
5	8,810	9,063	12,593	19,474
6	7,343	7,595	11,212	21,909
7	6,274	6,582	11,309	25,761
8	5,516	5,787	10,774	27,934
9	4,899	5,087	10,579	30,569
10	4,472	4,661	10,654	33,161

bonds with three neighboring Methodists. She is then at risk of defecting from the Process and becoming a Methodist. If she follows differential association theory on her next turn, and the Methodists have not in the meantime broken off their ties with her, then she definitely will convert to Methodism. This reminds us that in the real world, outreach techniques can have the opposite effect from the intended conversion of nonmembers, namely, the defection of members. Within this simulation, both processes will take place, and which predominates will depend upon the social and denominational structure of the community around the group that is practicing outreach.

Table 4.4 shows the growth of a group practicing outreach, depending upon the number of denominations in the community. The simulation always begins with a randomly determined distribution of denominations and social bonds across a network with approximately 50 percent density. On a given turn, each agent has a 50 percent probability of following balance theory rather than differential association theory. For one denomination only, if the agent follows balance theory the agent then has a 50 percent chance of subsequently engaging in outreach.

The first row of figure in table 4.4 shows a run in which a denomination practicing outreach is competing with only one other denomination that does not practice it. By chance, the outreach denomination starts with 22,043 members, just insignificantly less than half the 44,100 population of Cyburg. After 1 turn, membership has grown to just slightly over half, 22,279 members. (It is worth noting that a "turn" means that the computer selects an agent at random 44,100 times, but this does not mean that each agent gets a turn; some may miss a turn while others get two or more turns. Randomness intrudes everywhere in human affairs.) After 10 turns, however, the group's population has dropped to 21,650, and after fully 100 turns to 18,326. This is another example of chaotic behavior. Other runs under the same conditions show the outreach group growing slightly. With only one competing denomination of equal size, outreach appears to have no net advantage or disadvantage. But complex random events can produce growth or decline in any dynamic system.

When the outreach denomination faces two or more equal-sized competitors, however, outreach become an advantage—increasingly so as the total number of denominations increases from 3 to 10. In the case of 10 denominations, the outreach group grows slightly from 4,472 members to 4,661 over the first turn, then more than doubles to 10,654 members at 10 turns, and to more than 7 times its original size and a majority of Cyburg residents with 33,161 members after 100 turns. Ironically, it would seem that starting small is an advantage for a group that wants to grow. But in this set of simulations, that is true only because all the groups are the same size, and small size reflects religious pluralism.

This establishes an interesting point: Religious pluralism provides fertile ground for a religious group to grow. Thus, it would seem that pluralism contains the seeds of its own destruction, because it helps some groups absorb others, thereby reducing the degree of pluralism. Religious pluralism would naturally decay into religious monopoly, were it not for processes of schism and innovation that create new movements (Stark and Bainbridge 1985).

One might wonder why growth takes so long. At any given moment, only a few nonmembers are ripe for recruitment by a group practicing outreach. Recruiting some of them opens up new territory for recruiting others, step by step. As anyone who has played chess or checkers knows, if your opponent captures one of your pieces, then some other one of your pieces may become vulnerable even if it was not vulnerable previous to your opponent's move. We have no good metric for measuring the speed of the simulations in terms of clock time in the real world. Clearly, many people in real life never convert even once during their lifetimes, and few convert more than once. Presumably, volatility of religious affiliation is a variable, and this simulation suggests one of the factors that can increase it is religious pluralism.

MISCELLANEOUS FACTORS SHAPING CONVERSION
Our simulations gain clarity by being simple, but it is technically possible to include a very large number of factors in a simulation. Here we will re-run the previous simulation under five different conditions, duplicating the

last run, adding three factors one at a time, and adding all three factors at once. These factors have all been mentioned in the scientific literature and concern (1) psychological commitment, (2) social isolation, and (3) cultural continuity.

The social-scientific perspective variously called *rational choice, behaviorism,* or *learning theory* has always been skeptical of the idea that individuals become committed psychologically to a set of beliefs, quite apart from the contingencies of reward and social influence that reinforce commitment (Scott 1971). Nonetheless, internalization of faith appears regularly in the writings of religious scholars, and there is no reason to exclude it from examination. Indeed, its converse appears in the Lofland-Stark model: A religious seeker is precisely noncommitted to his or her original religion, and someone at a turning point may be unusually free psychologically to convert.

To this point, the simulations of this chapter have given no weight to the individual agent's current religious affiliation in the differential association process. If a Baptist, say, had two Baptist friends, and three Methodist friends, the person would convert to Methodism because three outnumber two. There are many ways to model religious faith, and the two concluding chapters of this book will offer a rather more complex one, but here we can model it simply by including the person's own affiliation in the count of the neighborhood. A Baptist with two Baptist friends counts as three Baptists in the neighborhood, able to fend off the social influence of three Methodists and leave the person unconverted and still a Baptist.

The first two rows of table 4.5 show a run with internalization switched off, just like the last run in table 4.4, and a run with internalization switched on. Again, there are 10 religious denominations, the agents follow balance theory half the time, and the group whose membership is shown in the table is the only denomination practicing outreach. We can see that internalization of

Table 4.5. Membership Growth as a Function of Three Special Rules

Special Rules in Effect	Members at Start	Members after 1 Turn	Members after 10 Turns	Members after 100 Turns
None	4,415	4,637	10,140	32,560
Internalized Commitment	4,458	4,580	5,015	13,524
Social Isolation	4,474	4,681	10,592	38,873
Internalized Commitment and Social Isolation	4,414	4,548	4,991	14,464
Cultural Continuity	4,460	4,489	5,039	5,407

commitment among potential converts slows down but does not stop conversion by the outreach group.

The third row of figures in table 4.5 has social isolation switched on and internalized commitment switched off. On rare occasions (actually 5 percent of the time, because balance theory is set to only 50 percent of the time and isolation occurs at a rate of 10 percent when balance theory is in effect), an agent loses all social bonds, becoming ripe pickings for any outreach group that happens to be in the neighborhood. This illustrates the part of the Lofland-Stark model that says a person is liable to convert when "attachments are absent or neutralized." Indeed, the outreach group grows more quickly than in any of the other conditions.

The fourth row combines both internal commitment (which retards conversion) with social isolation (which encourages conversion), and it shows a result intermediate between the two rules applied singly. This reminds us that real life involves many often competing factors, the causal effects of which can be disentangled only with difficulty by elaborate statistical analysis. In computer simulation, we can see the separate and combined effects of many factors by experimentally switching them on and off.

The final row of figures introduces cultural continuity. As Stark (1996b, 136) has hypothesized, "New religious movements are likely to succeed to the extent that they retain cultural continuity with the conventional faith(s) of the societies in which they seek converts." Here we are concerned not with the faith of the society, but of the potential convert, and can suggest: *An individual is more likely to convert to a religious organization that has a culture similar to his or her current affiliation.* Other factors may oppose this proposition. For example, a highly frustrated person may experience so much psychological tension that he or she is ready to take an especially long leap of faith. But other things being equal, cultural continuity can be expected to lower the barrier to conversion: there is less to learn, less to unlearn, and less additional belief to bear.

In this simulation, we model cultural continuity by imagining that the 10 denominations are numbered in a cultural spectrum from 1 to 10, with adjacent groups like 5 and 6 being highly similar, and 1 and 10 being very different. When continuity is switched on, a group may convert only from numerically adjacent groups. The group given the outreach capability happens to be Denomination 1, so it can recruit only from Denomination 2, and this severely limits its pool of potential recruits. Over a hundred turns, it grows by nearly 1,000 members, but remains far smaller than under any of the other conditions. In the real world, many groups may be more or less similar to a recruiting group, and there may be some slim probability of gaining a recruit from any cultural background. Nonetheless, it is important to realize—and to model in simulations—the fact that any religious movement has a somewhat limited pool of potential converts.

The final simulation for this chapter is not shown in the table, because it gives four different denominations the power of outreach, while having the cultural continuity rule in effect. These are Denominations 1, 4, 7, and 10. As usual, the average denomination membership at the beginning of the run is about 4,410 (10 percent of Cyburg's population). After 100 turns, the four denominations having the benefit of outreach achieve average memberships of 5,938, compared with 3,392 for the six other groups. However, Denominations 4 and 7, being able to recruit from two other denominations, did best, having 6,524 and 6,523 members respectively. Denominations 1 and 10 could recruit only from one other denomination, because they stood at the very extremes of the religious spectrum, so they achieved only 5,455 and 5,248 members.

SUMMATION

This chapter has begun to give the simulated agents much more complex decisions to make, although it has not yet endowed them with real autonomy. Each agent operates probabilistically, selecting among very clearly defined rules for behavior. Much of the intelligence remains at the social level, and the simulation outcomes emerge from interactions among large numbers of relatively simpleminded agents. However, when all the options are switched on, each agent has as many as three distinct decisions to make each turn (balance versus differential association, outreach versus not, isolation versus not), in a rather complex social environment that shapes the consequences of these decisions.

As Stark and I suggested a quarter-century ago, much about religious conversion can be explained entirely in terms of social networks and the dynamics of changing social bonds. In full awareness that other factors can also be important, we can see that computer simulations are an especially good method for exploring the theoretical implications of various propositions about dynamic social networks.

Considering only the social influence effects, religious pluralism can reduce religious mobilization, leading to a reduction in the density of the social network and an increase in the number of social isolates and the unchurched. However, once religious conversion enters the picture—for example, through the influence of differential association—social cohesion, and religious mobilization increase at the local level. Practicing outreach allows a group to grow, purely by reason of social-network effects, and religious pluralism is an especially good environment for growth by means of social recruitment.

5

Trust

The simulations described in this chapter will employ a simple but effective neural network algorithm that illustrates common principles of this class of computational tools. Designed for use in a range of simulation studies, this Minimum Intelligent Neural Device (MIND) is capable of learning which of a complex set of stimuli to avoid, and large numbers of these devices can be assembled in programs to explore the development of religious prejudice and of various interaction strategies. To give the simulations contemporary relevance, we will imagine that Cyburg lies somewhere near the Middle East—Lebanon or Bosnia, for example—where Christians and Muslims live together. We will explore the impact on group relations if a fundamentalist sect of angry young Muslim men starts causing trouble, in a context where the wicked Christian king uses the church to oppress his people. Perhaps the trouble is well deserved, and perhaps in a different context the tables would be turned and the established church would serve other interests. The scenario of this chapter is meant merely to provide a vivid story that illustrates the dynamics of the simulations.

NEURAL NETWORKS

Neural networks are computer programs designed by analogy with the network of neurons in human or animal brains, and they are one of the main methods for accomplishing machine learning. In truth, artificial neural nets, even simple ones, often are more analogous to connections between major modules in the brain, rather than between single neurons. Whatever the best analogy might be, neural nets are error-reduction algorithms with the potential to perform a wide range of useful tasks, including modeling theories of the social consequences of human error.

Humans learn from experience but have limited capacity to abstract correct rules from their experience. Gordon Allport (1954, 173) suggested that much prejudice results from a principle of least effort that affects the way humans categorize, and he said that "monopolistic categories are easier to form and to hold than are differentiated categories." This has affinities with the much more recent cognitive science theory of styles of religion proposed by Harvey Whitehouse (2004; Whitehouse and Laidlaw 2004; Whitehouse and Martin 2004; cf. Boyer 2002), based on the observation that some kinds of ideas are much easier to remember than others. In effect, Allport proposed a theory of error, and it should be possible to model this, employing neural networks.

We would need an artificial mind capable of differentiating categories of people but with some tendency to oversimplify. Then we would present it with a large number of stimulus persons, some of whom behave in an unpleasant (costly) manner. We would then look to see if the mind is overgeneralizing and reacting negatively to persons in categories factually separate from the ones containing misbehaving individuals.

Although mathematicians and computer scientists have worked with neural nets at least since the late 1940s, *back propagation* and other techniques that transformed them into versatile tools were not developed until the 1980s. This chapter demonstrates a particular neural network algorithm that can perform useful work in simulations of social interaction and that serves as the first step toward understanding the class of neural net algorithms that employs back propagation.

A back-propagation neural net is a learning device that can be taught to respond in a desired manner to a training set of data, and then used to analyze other data of the same kind. In training, the net is sequentially presented with a set of input and output vectors. In this context, *vector* refers to a meaningful set of structured data or information that can be entered into the net. At each step, one input vector is presented. Based on internal calculations, the net emits a response. This response is compared to the desired output vector, and any difference between these two is the error. This error is then propagated back through the network, adjusting values inside the net called *weights* or *connection strengths*, in such a way that the error would be smaller the next time the same input vector was presented. A properly designed neural net can model any continuous function whatsoever, and when applied to quantitative data, the accuracy of neural nets competes satisfactorily with more traditional analysis techniques such as multiple regression (Garson 1991; Huntley 1991; Smith 1993).

Because neural nets are learning devices that can handle error dynamically, they are good tools for representing human learning, decision making, and social interaction in multi-agent computer simulations. The standard goal in ordinary statistical analysis of empirical data is to avoid error, or at least to isolate and minimize the error terms in the equations, so quantitative sociologists are not in the habit of thinking about error as something that can have positive uses. But it is clear that sociology is deeply interested in the errors that human beings commit, and all human action takes place in contexts of incomplete information, cross-purposes, and random events that can magnify the importance of error. Hinton, Plaut, and Shallice (1993) have shown that neural nets can accurately model linguistic errors caused by physical damage to human brains, and a number of authors have drawn parallels between the problems solved by neural nets and the issues faced in psychiatry (Stein and Lidik 1998). While sociologists are primarily concerned with very different sources of error, the work in cognitive science suggests the potential that neural nets may have.

MIND was specifically designed to be a neural network that could solve complex problems but also make mistakes, such as becoming prejudiced against some people because it fails to fully understand the social situation. To see how MIND works, we will examine a simplified version of it in an abstract setting, and then we shall explore how a larger version of it functions in complex social interaction by giving each resident of Cyburg a MIND.

THE TINIEST MIND

To start with, we shall imagine four religious groups. Two of them are Christian, and two of them are Islamic. In each tradition, there is a low-tension church or mosque, and a high-tension sect. An agent whose mental apparatus consists of MIND meets a number of people, at random, from these four groups. If the interaction is pleasant, MIND should learn to accept the person. If it is unpleasant, MIND should learn to reject the person and refuse to interact with him or her. Thus, the agent will learn to seek rewarding experiences with pleasant exchange partners, and to avoid costly interactions with people who belong to a group that has proven obnoxious in the past.

On the input side, this scenario has two dichotomous variables, Christian versus Islamic and low-tension church (or mosque) versus high-tension sect. There is one dichotomous output: accept or reject. MIND codes these as binary numbers:

Input 1: Islamic = 0; Christian = 1

Input 2: low-tension = 0; high-tension = 1

Output: accept = 0; reject = 1

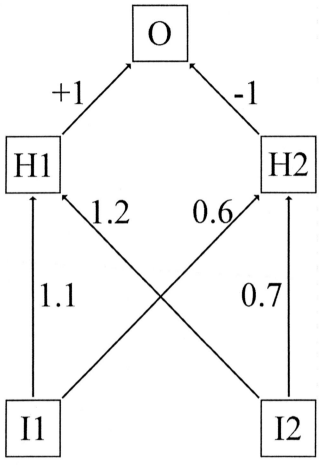

FIGURE 5.1
A Simple Neural Network

Thus, the net needs two inputs and one output. Figure 5.1 diagrams a simplified version, with the two inputs at the bottom (I1, I2), and the output (O) at the top. Each person the agent encounters is encoded as a two-bit number:

00 = Islamic low-tension

01 = Islamic high-tension

10 = Christian low-tension

11 = Christian high-tension

Considered as a "black box," the net works as follows. It receives a stimulus consisting of a 2-bit binary number (00, 01, 10, 11, equivalent to 0–3 in the decimal system). It responds with either 0 or 1. In terms of our scenario, an output of 0 could be interpreted as acceptance of another person who is described by the stimulus, and 1 as rejection or hostility.

The environment then returns to MIND a one-bit message telling MIND whether it responded correctly or incorrectly. Over a series of inputs, MIND learns to avoid errors. Afterward, if the environmental contingencies change, MIND will adjust to respond to these new contingencies. Thus, there is not necessarily a distinction here, as there is in much neural net statistical work, between a training set of data and the analysis set.

The environmental contingencies can be quite complex. If the Islamic sect engages in obnoxious behavior, the net needs to learn to respond 0 to inputs of 00, 10, and 11, but respond 1 to an input of 01. Perhaps instead the low-tension Christian church supports a tyrannical king, who oppresses all his subjects. Then the net should respond 0 to inputs of 00, 01, and 11, but respond 1 to an input of 10. Unfortunately for Cyburg, both these unpleasant things may be true, and both low-tension Christianity and high-tension Islam are obnoxious. In this case, the net should respond 0 to accept both 00 and 11, and respond 1 to reject both 01 and 10. This last example requires the net to learn what is called the *exclusive or operator* (XOR). An influential early book about neural networks (Minsky and Papert 1969) claimed they could not solve this problem, contributing to a 15-year loss of interest in neural nets until researchers in the 1980s invented nets that could handle this problem perfectly well.

The secret in designing neural nets that function well is what lies between the input and the output: one or more layers of hidden units. Without one of these layers of neuron-like components, a net cannot solve XOR, but with a sufficient number of them there may be no limit to the computable problems it can solve. MIND was actually constructed with 4 inputs and 4 hidden units, so it can handle the problems encountered later in this chapter. Figure 5.1 shows a somewhat simpler neural net with only two inputs and two hidden units, so we can see how such devices function.

As with most neural networks, information about the correct response to a particular stimulus is not placed in a single memory register or bank of registers dedicated to that stimulus alone, but is distributed across a set of memory registers shared by other pieces of information. These registers represent connections between the input and the output, via the hidden units, and the numbers stored in them are called *weights*. In figure 5.1, there are four weights between the input and hidden units: 1.1, 1.2, 0.6, and 0.7. There are also two weights between the hidden units and the output, $+1$ and -1.

We can think of each hidden unit as analogous to a nerve, with the weights being its connections to other nerves. In a way that will be explained shortly, the hidden units "vote" whether the output unit should put out a 1 or 0. Each hidden unit is turned on or off by the combination of inputs through the four weights reaching it. In this particular very simple net, if a "1" comes into a particular input unit, it passes on to the two hidden units the weights that connect it to them. The technical way to say this is that weights are "active" only if the associated input is 1. If a "0" comes in, nothing happens. For example, if the input is 10, input I1 gets the 1 and therefore sends 1.1 to H1 and 0.6 to H2. The other input, I2, receives the zero in 10, and so it does nothing.

If the input number were 11, then both I1 and I2 would send forward their respective weights, and the hidden units would add the numbers they receive together. H1 would receive 1.1 from I1 and 1.2 from I2, adding them together to get 2.3. H2 would receive 0.6 from I1 and 0.7 from I2 to get 1.3. If the sum of numbers reaching a hidden unit is greater than 1.0, it will send information on to the output unit. If the sum is less than or equal to 1, it will not. Therefore, with an input of 11, both H1 and H2 "fire" (to use neurological slang). This means they pass a number on to the output. For H1, the number sent to the output is $+1$, while for H2, it is -1.

If the sum of numbers coming from the hidden units to the output is 1, the output puts out 1. If the sum of these numbers is 0 or -1, the output is 0. H2 can be called an "inhibitor," by analogy with inhibitor neurons in neurobiology. If H2 fires, it sends -1 to output, forcing the output to be 0. H1, in contrast, is an "excitor." If H1 fires, it sends $+1$ to the output. The output will be 1 if and only 1 H1 fires but H2 does not fire. Otherwise, the output will be 0. Note that this net solves XOR, because it responds with a 1 to inputs of both 10 and 01, but responds 0 to 11 and 00.

This general type of neural net learns by adjusting the connection weights in response to errors. This tiny neural net has a serious limitation, because it cannot be given weights between the input and hidden units that would allow it to respond 1 to an input of 00. The slightly larger net used in our simulations handles this by having 4 hidden units, 2 that are activated by an input of 1—one excitor and one inhibitor—and 2 that are activated by an input of

0—again, one excitor and one inhibitor (Bainbridge 1995a). Artificial intelligence researchers have developed a very large variety of neural nets, and they often design them so that the weights between the hidden units and the output are also adjusted during learning. Omitting that feature from MIND is one of the intentional limitations that gives it an appropriate balance between accurate learning and error, suitable for the present research, while incorporating the realistic neurological distinction between excitors and inhibitors.

At the beginning of a computer run, all the weights are set to 0.000. If the net responds correctly to a given stimulus, nothing is done to the weights. But if it responds incorrectly, the program seeks out every active weight that might be wrong and adjusts it in what might be the right direction. The amount the weight changes is a product of a "learning rate" and a random real number in the range 0.0 to 1.0.

If a hidden unit behaved properly, the weights connected to it are left alone. That is, if the output should have been 1, and HI fired, the weights connected to H1 are left alone. But if H1 did not fire, which implies that some of the weights may have been too small, each of the active weights to H1 is increased. In contrast, if the output was supposed to be 0, but it was 1 and H1 fired, each of the active weights to H1 will be reduced.

The "learning rate" is 0.2 for the MIND net, a number that was empirically derived. If the learning rate is too low, the net takes a long time to learn. If it is too high, the net can become unstable. Moderate instability is not necessarily a bad thing, because it can help the net escape *local minima*, which are suboptimal solutions that are better than other very similar solutions, but worse than some very different solutions. Local minima are actually very interesting, because they represent a very human quality: a reluctance to give up beliefs that function pretty well at the cost of never finding the real truth. One way of expressing the thesis of this book is to say: *Religious faith is a local minimum.*

LEARNING TO OVERCOME PREJUDICE

Now we shall imagine that Cyburg is frequently visited by members of 16 religious groups, whether proselytizing or merely doing personal business, with all possible combinations of four dichotomous characteristics:

Input 1: Islamic = 0; Christian = 1

Input 2: low-tension = 0; high-tension = 1

Input 3: old group = 0; new group = 1

Input 4: politically uninvolved = 0; politically involved = 1

In addition to the religious tradition (Islamic versus Christian) and degree of tension with the sociocultural environment (low-tension church or mosque versus high-tension sect), we now have old, well-established groups versus new religious movements, and groups that differ in terms of how much they engage in political activity. This is a wide range of variations, and later we will take advantage of it. With four inputs and hidden units, MIND is in fact capable of handling many problems involving all four variables, although it finds some problems extremely challenging. Here, we shall limit our focus just to the first two variables, in two simulations.

In the first simulation, residents of Cyburg are going to find people from low-tension Christian groups obnoxious, as we suggested because they are connected to the distant but oppressive king. In the second simulation, they will continue to reject low-tension Christian strangers visiting their town, but they will also reject high-tension Islamic visitors. Here, the denominations of the Cyburg residents will not matter. They are not relating to each other, as they will in a later simulation, but to the strangers in their midst. Our first research question is to compare how quickly they learn to respond correctly for each of these problems, predicting that the more complex second problem will take them longer.

The simulation proceeds in a series of rounds, until all 44,100 residents of Cyburg have solved the given problem. In each round, each resident gets a turn. In that turn, the agent meets 16 people, each of who has one of the possible 16 combinations of characteristics: 0000, 0001, 0010, 0011, 0100, 0101, 0110, 0111, 1000, 1001, 1010, 1011, 1100, 1101, 1111. Importantly, the agent does not necessarily meet 16 people with all 16 possibilities. The agent could meet three with the same characteristic combinations, and none with some other combinations. This is important because it assures that different residents of the town will have somewhat different experiences, and thus will learn at somewhat different rates.

Each time the agent meets one of these strangers, the neural net takes in the stranger's characteristics and either accepts or rejects the stranger. If the response was correct—in the first simulation rejecting low-tension Christians but accepting everybody else—no learning take place. However, if the response was incorrect, either rejecting when the agent should have accepted, or vice versa, the error is propagated back into the net, changing the connection weights as described above.

After each round, the computer tests all the agents by presenting each of them with all 16 stimuli, to see how they react. No learning takes place in this test; it is merely a way of collecting data on the current performance of each agent. In particular, the test counts how many errors of each kind the agent commits.

For these experiments, only two of the four input variables are significant. It does not matter whether the stranger belongs to a politically active group or a new one. Thus the net needs to ignore half of the information it gets, and focus on the other half of the information that is salient for the particular problem. Another way of putting it is that the agent needs to place all the low-tension Christians in the same category: 1000, 1001, 1010, and 1011, if the first two bits in the series of four need to be 10.

In fact, all the agents eventually learn to make the correct judgments, in both of these simulations, some more quickly than others. Figure 5.2 graphs the rising number of agents who have solved their problem and have stopped committing errors. The last agent solves the 10 problem on round 26; the last agent solves the 10 & 01 problem on round 93. Thus the curve for the 10 problem jumps up to its limit (44,100 error-free agents) very quickly, compared with the more sluggish curve for 10 & 01.

This is pure trial-and-error learning, and humans might learn more quickly, especially if they discuss their experiences with each other. However, introducing language would bring with it all kinds of other sources of prejudice, and muddy the clarity of the experiment. It is worth noting that subjects had to meet many people to gain enough experience to solve the problems. At the beginning of both experiments, all agents made mistakes, because they were initially prepared to accept everybody and had to learn to reject. In the first experiment (learning to reject low-tension Christians), 69 residents of Cyburg became error-free after two rounds. That means they solved the problem somewhere between 16 and 32 encounters with strangers. The last agent to solve the problem needed at least 400 encounters.

Perhaps more interesting than the number of errors is their kind. Failing to reject a stranger who belongs to the obnoxious group (as defined by the experimenter) is a false negative error. Rejecting a stranger who does not belong

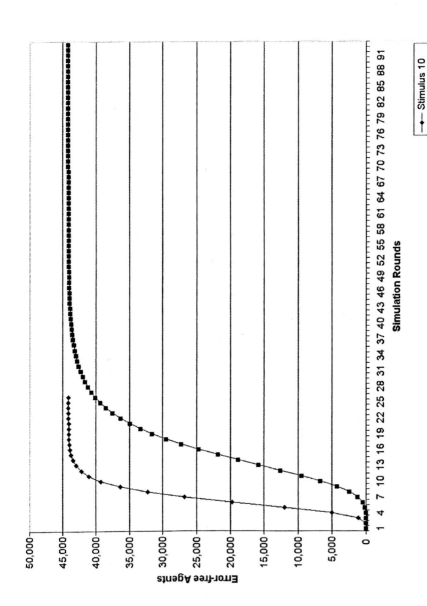

FIGURE 5.2
Neural Net Error Reduction.

Table 5.1. Prejudice against 16 Sects and Denominations

Group Judged	Simulation 1 (10) Errors		Simulation 2 (10 & 01) Errors	
	False Negative	False Positive	False Negative	False Positive
0000		3,086		130
0001		883		1,363
0010		855		1,294
0011		153		5,567
0100		2	4,804	
0101		0	2,168	
0110		0	2,202	
0111		1	4,949	
1000	3,646		4,882	
1001	3,030		2,055	
1010	2,975		2,143	
1011	3,655		4,939	
1100		201		5,762
1101		880		1,380
1110		888		1,435
1111		3,039		146
Total	13,306	9,988	28,142	17,077

to an obnoxious group is a false positive. The latter is what we often mean by prejudice, treating somebody negatively because of a false belief we have in our minds. During the middle of the learning period, agents might tend to make errors of both kinds, but some problems might produce a greater proportion of prejudicial false positives.

Table 5.1 shows the distributions of errors across stimuli at about the middle of both simulation runs, during the round in which half the population of the town solved the particular problem. In the first simulation, 26,826 agents had solved the 10 problem by the end of round 7. In the second simulation, 24,694 agents had solved the 10 & 01 problem by the end of round 16.

In both simulations, there were fewer false positive (prejudiced) reactions than false negatives. This results from the fact that the agents started out primed to accept a stranger before their learning began, rather than to reject strangers. An initial openness to others—call it *friendliness* if this is not too anthropomorphic—features in some of the simulations and related research described in the next chapter, as well. Nevertheless, we see large numbers of prejudicial false positives, 9,988 and 17,077. Interestingly, the innocent groups that suffer worst in the first simulation, 0000 and 1111, fare best in the second simulation. This is a nice illustration of significant facts about human prejudice: False beliefs can have surprising negative consequences, and prejudicial ideologies vary in the particular patterns of harm they cause.

DIFFICULT COGNITIVE CHALLENGES

We have just seen that it took residents of Cyburg longer to solve the more complex problem of simulation 2 than the easy problem of simulation 1. Now we will present them with even more difficult problems, ratcheting the cognitive challenge up near the point at which learning breaks down altogether. Simulation 3 is the same as simulation 2, except that a third obnoxious group starts proselytizing, one that is Christian, high-tension, new, and politically activist. Its binary code, therefore, is 1111. So, in simulation 3, the agents have to learn to reject all groups that start with 10 and 01, plus the group 1111, but accept all others.

In fact, this is a difficult problem for MIND, although a solvable one, and the last agent does not solve it until round 311, after encountering more than 4,910 strangers. More than half of the agents, 22,508 of them, had solved the problem by the end of round 39, and table 5.2 shows the distribution of errors

Table 5.2. Prejudice from Cognitive Difficulty

Group Judged	Simulation 3 (10 & 01 & 1111) Errors		Simulation 4 (0001 & 0010 & 0100 & 0111) Errors	
	False Negative	False Positive	False Negative	False Positive
0000		284		8,626
0001		1,775	10,904	
0010		1,805	10,874	
0011		5,270		6,858
0100	5,772		10,821	
0101	3,170			6,842
0110	3,192			6,920
0111	1,909		8,746	
1000	5,673			1
1001	3,316			0
1010	3,206			0
1011	2,054			35
1100		4,898		0
1101		5,058		41
1110		5,057		46
1111	11,485			11
Total	39,777	15,013	41,345	29,380

at that point. The agents who had not yet solved the problem were actually not making many errors. The total of 21,592 error-committing agents made 54,790 errors in the test after round 39, an average of just 2.54 each. Put the other way around, on average the error-committing agents get 13.46 of the 16 judgments right, or about 84 percent. If this were a school test, they would get a B, which is a passing grade. Thus, even though they have not perfectly solved the problem, they are handling it pretty well. This, I believe, is extremely realistic. Humans seldom, if ever, find perfect solutions to life's problems, but most people muddle through with satisfactory, suboptimal solutions.

As before, the table shows that prejudicial (false positive) errors are less common, again because the agents started the experiment with a predisposition to accept rather than reject strangers. Had we started them off with a xenophobic disposition, for example, by initializing each excitor connection weight at 0.5 rather than 0.0, they would have committed more false positive errors. Again, the errors are not evenly distributed. The error-committing agents fail to reject 1111 about half the time (false negative), and perhaps the same misconception causes them to reject 0000 less often than other false positive errors they make.

The final simulation with strangers, before we turn to one in which the agents are again interacting with each other, has a very serious scenario. At the time of this writing, a so-called War Against Terror is waging between the United States and some allies on one side, and a diffuse collection of high-tension Islamic movements on the other side. We have no way of knowing how long this situation will persist, but there have been somewhat comparable conflicts in the past, such as the River War of the early 1890s, when British Major-General Horatio Herbert Kitchener lead a small Anglo-Egyptian army up the Nile to avenge the death of Charles Gordon and regain the Sudan from "Mahdi" Mohammed Ahmed (Churchill 1902; Arthur 1920; Warner 1985). An issue that is not debated very openly or intelligently today is the extent to which the enemy of the West is Islam (cf. Huntington 1996), and it seems strategically very important for the West now as it was in Kitchener's day to define the enemy as only the most radical Islamic groups, in order to gain allies among moderate Muslims. Yet some Americans may feel that the enemy really is the whole of Islam, and the point of simulation 4 in this chapter is to explore how that belief could be a simple cognitive error.

As we have set up the scenario, there are 8 Islamic groups that have some contact with Cyburg: 0000, 0001, 0010, 0011, 0100, 0101, 0110, 0111. Let us imagine that four of these actually are obnoxious: 0001, 0010, 0100, and 0111. The other four are quite innocuous: 0000, 0011, 0101, and 0110. This simulation challenges the agents to learn to accept the four innocuous Islamic groups, and reject the four obnoxious Islamic groups. As might be expected, this is a very difficult problem for the limited cognitive abilities of MIND.

Figure 5.3 shows how many agents solved the problem on each of the first 50 rounds. Some agents solve the problem very quickly, already 7 of them by the end of round 2. Fully 155 solved it on the next round, 666 on round 4, 1,052 on round 5, and 1,228 on round 6, the largest number on any one round. Then the rate of solving it drops rapidly, down to 196 on round 18, 120 on round 29, and 99 on round 50. The average number solving the problem on rounds 51–100 is 108. The average for the next sets of 100 rounds are 101–200 = 83; 201–300 = 55; 301–400 = 36; and rounds 401–500 = 24.

After round 500, when we stopped the computer run, 39,243 agents had solved the problem, which means that 4,857 had not. At a rate of 24 per 100 rounds, it would take another 20,200 rounds for everybody to solve the problem. But this is an underestimate for two reasons. First, as we just saw, the number of agents solving the problem per 100 rounds was declining, a natural result of the fact that the solution is probabilistic and the number who are still left to solve the problem is declining. Second, these numbers of rounds have risen into the range where they are no longer plausible estimates of human behavior, if only because they do not take account of the fact that human beings do not live forever.

How many strangers do we meet each day and interact with sufficiently to say that the interaction had been either rewarding or costly? Let me guess: 5. Of these, most will be tradespeople with whom the interaction is limited to an economic exchange. I would be surprised, even in a religiously charged environment, if the average person would have even as many as 1 religiously salient interaction with a stranger each day. Running the simulation for 500 rounds means that 4,857 agents had still failed to solve the problem after meeting $500 \times 16 = 8,000$ strangers. At one a day, that would take 22 years.

Perhaps the remarkable thing about figure 5.3 is not the long right-hand tail of the distribution that in principle extends many yards beyond the edge of the page, but the spike of rapid problem solution that takes place in the first dozen or so rounds. Round 12 is the last one on which more than 500 agents solve the problem—538 to be exact—and at that point 8,028 agents have the

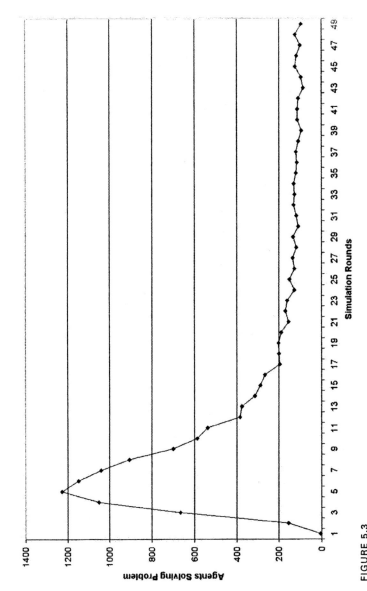

FIGURE 5.3

The Challenge of Distinguishing Islamic Groups.

solution. In a very real sense, the agents fall into two groups: about a fifth who solve the problem very quickly, and four-fifths who arrive at one or another false solution and stick with it until an unlikely sequence of encounters with strangers from just the right groups breaks them out of their false assumptions so they can learn the correct solution.

Table 5.2 shows the pattern of errors after round 127, when 22,106 agents had solved the problem. The remaining 21,994 agents made a total of 70,725 errors, or an average of about 3.2 each and about 80 percent correct judgments. Their 29,380 false positive errors are heavily concentrated on the innocent Islamic groups, who receive 99.5 percent of these prejudicial judgments. Only on very rare occasions was a Christian the victim of prejudice in this simulation. Thus, this prejudiced half of Cyburg had failed to distinguish innocuous Islamic groups from obnoxious ones, and stigmatized all of Islam.

AGENTS JUDGING EACH OTHER

To this point, we have imagined that the representatives of 16 religious groups were strangers visiting Cyburg, but in the two concluding simulations of this chapter we will change the simulation and the scenario so that the residents of Cyburg themselves are randomly assigned to these 16 sects and denominations. That means each group has an average size of 2,756.25 members, ranging by chance in simulation 5 from 2,647 to 2,869, and in simulation 6 from 2,678 to 2,856. As in simulation 4, the obnoxious groups are 0001, 0010, 0100, and 0111, representing half of the Islamic population of the town.

On a number of turns, the computer randomly selects pairs of residents and has them interact. Each sees the other's religious affiliation and reacts to it, by either acceptance or rejection. As in previous simulations of this chapter, over a large number of interactions the agents learn to distinguish the groups that should be accepted from those that should be rejected. Table 5.3 shows results after 1,000 turns, a number chosen to produce very nearly the same number of learning opportunities as the data from simulation 4 in table 5.3. This is a point at which about half of the residents have solved the problem, and the rest are stuck with suboptimal solutions and are only gradually escaping them.

This table is arranged differently from the other two, because each row represents the errors made by one of the 16 groups. Thus, members of 0000, an innocuous Islamic mosque, made 2,668 false negative errors, failing to reject one of the obnoxious groups, and 1,878 false positive (prejudicial) judgments.

Table 5.3. Prejudicial Behavior of 16 Sects and Denominations

Group Doing the Judging	Simulation 5: Can Reject Own Group		Simulation 6: Cannot Reject Own Group	
	False Negative	False Positive	False Negative	False Positive
0000	2,668	1,878	2,580	1,846
0001	2,520	1,684	422	277
0010	2,648	1,870	382	225
0011	2,684	1,756	2,563	1,935
0100	2,542	1,768	351	248
0101	2,686	1,894	2,613	1,787
0110	2,729	1,949	2,833	1,856
0111	2,600	1,727	0	4
1000	2,697	1,820	2,411	1,812
1001	2,629	1,752	2,676	1,787
1010	2,639	1,819	2,701	1,892
1011	2,691	1,870	2,520	1,703
1100	2,653	1,932	2,636	1,950
1101	2,669	1,770	2,537	1,825
1110	2,660	1,836	2,611	1,888
1111	2,631	1,990	2,740	1,887

Not very different are the scores of group 0010, an obnoxious Muslim sect: 2,648 false negatives and 1,870 false positives.

It is worth noting that in this simulation Islamic residents are just as prejudiced against fellow Muslims as the Christians are against them. Islamic residents committed 14,526 false positive errors, and fully 99.4 percent of them were against Muslims. Among Christian residents, 99.5 percent of the 14,789 prejudicial errors were against Muslims. The lack of a significant difference in anti-Muslim prejudice between Muslims and Christians should not be surprising, because this simulation does not factor the agent's own affiliation into the learning process. But there is at least a hint of realism here, because minorities often have to struggle with a measure of self-hatred to the extent they have internalized the culture of a dominant society that is prejudiced against them.

This simulation primarily illustrates the fact that we are technically able to endow interacting members of a multi-agent system with MINDs capable of learning about each other in a process of social interaction. This ability will be central to all the simulations reported in the rest of this book. But if we want to arrive at new results, we will have to introduce a new factor, and the most logical one at this point is to incorporate the agent's own affiliation in the learning process.

A simple way to do this in the present series of simulations is to focus on what happens when two members of the same sect or denomination interact with each other. Arguably, members of the same group do not find each other obnoxious, however obnoxious members of other groups may find them. The members of Al Qaeda who crashed into the World Trade Center and Pentagon on September 11, 2001, were a high-solidarity group. As Allen (1965) showed in his study of recruitment to the Nazi Party, a key factor in the growth of the movement was the development of bonds of friendship and trust among members. Just because the reader may not like members of Al Qaeda or the Nazis does not means that the members of such groups feel the same way about fellow members.

Simulation 6 is identical to simulation 5, except that it is not an error for members of an obnoxious group to accept other members of the same group. Members of 0001 should still reject members of 0010—we have not introduced solidarity across Islamic groups—but members of 0001 should accept other members of 0001, and members of 0010 should accept fellow 0010 members. After 1,000 turns, the results look very much the same for the innocuous groups, but the contrast could hardly be greater for the obnoxious ones.

Basically, by removing themselves from their learning process, members of high-solidarity obnoxious groups face a much easier cognitive problem than everybody else does. By 1,000 turns, nearly all of the members of these four Islamic groups have solved the problem of distinguishing people who should be accepted from those who should be rejected. The situation for members of Islamic sect 0111 is especially remarkable. They needed to learn to reject only members of 0001, 0010, and 0100, which apparently is a relatively simple problem for MIND. They made only 4 errors, all of them prejudicial false positives. For members of group 0001, the problem of learning to reject only 0010, 0100, and 0111 is somewhat harder, simply because of the location of the groups in the classification system.

I do not know how important this discovery is, but analogs may exist in the real world. Certainly people situated in different locations in society have different perspectives. In the modern, information-intensive world, access to information is both crucial and stratified. If one particular group constitutes much of the complexity in the social landscape, members of it may live in a simpler world if they are so comfortable with themselves to take themselves for granted. This may give them an advantage in competition with other groups, for purely cognitive reasons.

SUMMATION

We have taken the first steps to give the agents in our simulated community real, individual intelligence. We have seen how a minimal neural net works, and shown that it can be used to learn judgments about categorizing people. Fundamentally, the net takes a four-bit binary number, like 0111, and reduces it to a 1-bit number, 0 or 1. Thus, the job performed in these six simulations is really learning how to collapse categories properly. Other neural nets may have many outputs—in some cases as many outputs as inputs—but much of machine learning in computer science is primarily about classification of patterns in data.

The MIND neural net, of course, is far simpler than the brain of any insect, and it works only because the computer program and our verbal scenarios prepare much of the information for it. Consider how the agents identify the religious affiliations of the people they meet: they merely accept the bits of a 4-bit binary number into the appropriate inputs. With great effort and money, we could create a neural-net artificial intelligence system to do that classification in a fully automatic manner. A voice-recognition dialog system could interview the person, asking questions about religion. A computer vision system, many of which are based on neural nets, could look at the person's clothing, and make inferences based on the presence or absence of a beard or a turban. Even without such "bells and whistles," MIND can be a useful tool for theorizing about prejudice and the interactions between religious sects and denominations.

The very simplicity of theory-based computer simulations can be a great advantage. Here, we have successfully illustrated Allport's cognitive effort theory of prejudice. It assumes that different groups in society really do have different characteristics, and members of some groups may tend (at least statistically) to offend members of other groups. A truly wise response to such a situation is to understand it well enough so that one can make fair judgments, based on how people actually behave. Here, we have seen neural net agents acting prejudicially, because they had not yet solved the problem of learning how to distinguish obnoxious people from innocuous people who merely have some of the same characteristics.

This does not in any way diminish the validity of alternative theories, unless of course they are presented as the complete explanation for prejudice. However, this simulation does put those other theories under a little heavier empirical burden in the debate over the roots of prejudice. Sometimes a theory gains credence only because it presents a plausible story in the absence of any alternative. If our simulation shows an alternate way that results could come about, then the other theory is no longer quite so convincing in the absence of empirical data.

For example, one classic explanation for prejudice is the theory of the *authoritarian personality* (Adorno et al. 1950). Supposedly, some people have rigid, authoritarian personalities, whereas other are more flexible, liberal, and open to new experiences. Well, none of our 44,100 agents have more authoritarian or more flexible personalities than the others, nor did they differ in native intelligence, yet some quickly solved the problems and avoided prejudice, whereas others did not. Their different beliefs and behavior were entirely the result of different luck in the randomly determined sequences of stimuli they were presented with.

It would, in fact, be easy to add individual differences comparable to the authoritarian personality to this simulation, especially the variant of this theory that focuses on the difference between open and closed minds (Rokeach 1960). All the simulations in this chapter used a learning rate of 0.2—a constant that was multiplied by a random number between 0.0 and 1.0, to determine how much a given connection weight in a neural net would be changed during an episode of learning in response to error. We can vary that rate, say down to 0.1 or up to 0.5, either for all agents at once, or giving agents a range of different learning rates. A low learning rate represents a closed mind, and a high one represents an open mind. An agent with a low rate learns more slowly and may have much greater difficulty getting out of a suboptimal solution to the problem. On the other hand, a very high learning rate produces mental instability and at the extreme just as much inability to learn as does a learning rate of zero.

In this chapter, we have labeled members of some groups obnoxious, but we have not actually let them behave in an obnoxious manner. The next challenge will be to find a way in which the agents can learn how to deal with other people not on the basis of preordained labels, but on the basis of the actual behavior of those people.

6

Cooperation

Every religion promulgates some kind of moral code, from the Eight-Fold Path to the Ten Commandments, from "Do unto others as you would have them do unto you" to "Love thy neighbor as thyself." However, one of the major thrusts in social-scientific computer simulation research has been to explore how altruism, cooperation, or social benevolence might arise in society without religion or any kind of shared values, culture, or ethics. Much of this work builds on a classic game-theory problem about a situation that discourages cooperation.

RELIGION AND SOCIAL CONTROL

From ancient days until the present, people have assumed that a primary function of religion is to uphold morality, and there is an extensive social-scientific literature on how religion may reduce crime and other forms of deviant behavior (Bainbridge 1989a; Stark and Bainbridge 1996). The case is not so clear as we might like, and some of the presumed powers of religion to uphold morality may be illusory or spurious. For example, studies generally fail to find a negative correlation between the rate of church membership across communities and the homicide rate. Apparently, the commandment "Thou shalt not kill" is ineffective. On the other hand, there is a consistent negative correlation between the church member rate and the theft or larceny rate. "Thou shalt not steal" seems to be somewhat effective.

It may be that values are very weak things, capable of guiding people in situations of little emotional arousal and where deviant behavior offers only mild rewards. The very concept of "values" has come into question, especially the traditional ("structural-functional") sociological view that people and society possess coherent sets of values that are abstract principles capable of actually guiding life (Bainbridge 1994). Stark and I (1987) argued that values are cultural solutions to the problems of achieving innate human needs, but we preferred to call them *general explanations.*

Humans seek rewards and try to avoid costs. They rely not only upon their clever brains but also upon social constructions like language. To solve a problem means to imagine possible means of achieving the desired reward, to select the one with the greatest likelihood of success in the light of available information, and to direct action along the chosen line until the reward has been achieved. To solve problems, humans seek what Stark and I called *explanations*, but which more recently I have preferred to call *algorithms* (Bainbridge 2003). Norms are lesser algorithms, and values are greater algorithms—or *specific explanations* and *general explanations*, as Stark and I called them two decades ago (Stark and Bainbridge 1985, 1987). Under whatever name, these are instructions, recipes, plans, or strategies stating the nature of the problem and the means to solve it. Religion offers very general explanations for how to attain many of the most important rewards in life, including perhaps the transcendence of death itself. So it is at least plausible that religion deters some kinds of deviance merely by providing verbal advice to believers on the most advantageous strategies to follow. In particular, religion takes the long view, concerned less with immediate material rewards than with the entire course of life and what may lie beyond.

In our theory book (Stark and Bainbridge 1987, 99–100), we considered the way religious specialists (e.g., priests) had an implicit bargain with their followers concerning the flow of rewards, a topic I have reexamined more recently (Bainbridge 2002). Three of the numbered propositions in the theory book state the general idea.

P78 Religious specialists promulgate norms, said to come from the gods, that increase the rewards flowing to the religious specialists.
P79 Religious specialists promulgate norms, said to come from the gods, that increase the ability of their clients to reward the religious specialists.
P80 Religious specialists promulgate norms, said to come from the gods, that increase the total rewards possessed by the clients as a group.

Religion may have many influences on behavior, but one operates through the general algorithms it promulgates, affecting and probably increasing the ability of believers to gain rewards in everyday life, perhaps with an emphasis on those long-term goals that require sacrifice and patience, and thereby that may not readily be gained by following momentary desires or reacting to immediate opportunities. Thus, one of the many scientific approaches that should be followed in order to better understand the social function of religion is to examine the role it plays in supporting certain strategies of action. Here, we enter a multidisciplinary territory where sociology meets psychology, economics, and decision and risk studies, a field where computer simulations are standard tools for research.

THE HUMAN DILEMMA

For decades, laboratory psychologists noted that cooperation in humans and animals can arise from very simple social interactions (Sidowski, Wyckoff, and Tabory 1956; Kelley, Thibaut, Radloff, and Mundy 1962; cf. Miller and Dollard 1941). When game theory became popular in the 1960s in economics and international relations (Boudon 1981), it often returned to an intellectual puzzle called the Prisoner's Dilemma. Imagine this:

> Two men are suspected of having committed a crime together. They are placed in separate cells, and each is informed separately that he may choose to confess or not, subject to the following stipulations: (1) If both independently choose not to confess, they will receive only moderate punishment. (2) On the other hand, if one chooses not to confess and the other simultaneously confesses, the confessor will receive the minimal sentence while his partner will be given the maximal sentence. (3) If both choose to confess, they will both be given heavy sentences. (Gergen 1969, 54)

This situation is ironic and tragic. Each prisoner will think to himself as follows: "What if my partner confesses? If I keep silent, then I will get a worse sentence than if I confess, too. So, in that case, I would be better off confessing. What if he does not confess? Then I can get a very light sentence if I do confess. So, I should confess, no matter what he does."

This logic will convince both of the men to confess. But if both prisoners confess, they will get harsher sentences than if they both keep silent. This gives the seeming paradox that people acting logically in pursuit of their own personal interests will harm themselves. Indeed, even if they have read about the prisoner's dilemma and know the tragic implications of their situation, they will find it hard to trust the other to keep silent, and thus they will confess despite the ultimate harm it does them.

One answer could be that the prisoners could have previously sworn to keep silent, in the name of Almighty God. For believers, this alters the structure of the social situation by introducing a new agent, namely God, who will know what the men do and can punish oath violators. Throughout history are recorded great moments when people sought to invoke the supernatural to help people cooperate or at least to avoid harming each other. A classic example is the remarkable story, told by Xenophon (1998), of the Greek army that advanced to the very heart of the Persian empire, where they suddenly found themselves bereft of allies and desperately trying to escape with their lives. At several points in this true story, the Greeks parlayed with the Persians trying to arrange safe passage ensured by holy oaths.

Clearly, the story of the two prisoners depicts a situation where cooperation is very difficult, and supernatural intervention (or faith in it) might be needed. But many people find it artificial and even hard to visualize. Anatol Rapoport (1962; cf. Rapoport and Chammah 1965) noted that Puccini's grand opera *Tosca* contains an enactment of the same problem in different terms.

Tosca and Cavaradossi are in love. Tosca loathes the evil police chief Scarpia, but Scarpia is attracted to her. Cavaradossi has been condemned to death and is the prisoner of Scarpia, his archenemy. Tosca and Scarpia make a bargain. She agrees to submit to his romantic embraces. He agrees to stage a mock execution with blank cartridges and let Cavaradossi escape. But they double-cross each other. She stabs him, and he has slyly failed to save Cavaradossi from the firing squad.

A standard way to analyze exchanges in economic game theory is in terms of real or hypothetical payoffs from different actions under different circumstances. Analyzing the payoffs possible for Tosca and Scarpia, Rapoport showed how each was driven by rational calculation to double-cross the other. Table 6.1 shows the payoffs, using simpler numbers than Rapoport's. The precise payoff numbers are arbitrary. What matters is that certain payoffs are better than others.

Table 6.1. Payoffs in an Operatic Prisoner's Dilemma

	Tosca's Payoff		Scarpia's Payoff	
	Scarpia Keeps Bargain	Scarpia Double-crosses	Scarpia Keeps Bargain	Scarpia Double-crosses
Tosca Keeps Bargain	+1	−2	+1	+2
Tosca Double-crosses	+2	−1	−2	−1

Let's think things through from Tosca's viewpoint. Ideally, she would like to save Cavaradossi without submitting to Scarpia, and this happy outcome is represented by the +2 points in her payoff table if she double-crosses Scarpia while he keeps his bargain. The worst thing for her, represented by the −2, is if she submits to Scarpia but he double-crosses her, leaving Cavaradossi to die.

She does not know whether Scarpia has kept his word about the feigned execution or not. The first column of Tosca's payoff table shows what happens for her if Scarpia keeps his bargain. She does well, +1 point, if she also keeps her bargain. But she does better, +2, if she double-crosses him. The second column of figures in table 6.1 shows what happens if he double-crosses her. If she keeps her bargain, then she does very badly, −2, losing Cavaradossi and suffering from Scarpia's loathsome passions as well. But if she double-crosses him, she does not lose quite so much, −1. Thus, whatever he does, she is better off double-crossing him. So she does.

Scarpia's payoffs lead him to the same conclusion. Whether Tosca keeps her bargain or not, he does better by double-crossing her. Dying, with her dagger in his heart, he at least has the consolation that Cavaradossi dies too, a revenge motive that seems very compelling for characters in grand opera. And thus Tosca and Scarpia rationally chose behavior that gives them a worse outcome than if both had kept their bargains. Both received −1, while they could both have received +1.

George Homans (1950, 1974) was convinced that social norms can emerge from purely utilitarian motives, as individuals interact out of enlightened self-interest. He pointed out that the prisoner's dilemma assumed the men would never interact again for the rest of their lives. But, he noted, our most important social interactions are with people with whom we exchange again and again. Thus, Homans could imagine that religion was unnecessary to bring morality and cooperation into being, between people who interact repeatedly.

Homans was not by nature an irreligious man. Once, when we were walking our separate paths across Harvard Yard, I came up behind him and discovered he was singing the doxology to himself. As a social theorist, he believed very strongly that we should seek the simplest explanations of social behavior that are consistent with the facts. He was offended by the tendency of sociologists to bandy vague terms about, like *culture* and *values* (so Homans judged), when human behavior might more correctly be explained in terms of our biological heritage and a set of simple rules of social exchange between individuals. On a different day, our paths crossed again in Harvard Yard. George asked if I had read Robert Axelrod's (then) new book about the prisoner's dilemma, and the next day I did.

In *The Evolution of Cooperation*, Axelrod (1984) reported the results of a computer simulation in which the prisoner's dilemma was played over and over again by agents that could remember what their partner had done on the previous turn. This is called the *iterated prisoner's dilemma*. His computer program included many different strategies for playing the game, strategies that actually came from a public contest that Axelrod ran. Under many circumstances, the winning strategy was one contributed by Rapoport that could lead to cooperation if other agents were following the same strategy, but which could defend against being exploited by double-crossers. In Cyburg, we will begin by replicating Axelrod's experiment, then explore some of the ways that religion might possibly enhance the cooperative outcomes.

SEVEN STRATEGIES

We will begin our examination of cooperation using the prisoner's dilemma by restaging Axelrod's tournament in Cyburg, and then we will give the residents the power of machine learning. The first theoretical aim of these sets of simulations is to see how cooperation might arise without shared values such as those promulgated by religion, but then we will look at the possibility that religious values might help jump-start and sustain cooperation.

There will be seven different strategies for playing the iterated prisoner's dilemma, some more cooperative than others. Initially, for the Axelrod tournament, one strategy will be assigned to each group. Then we will do experiments with various combinations of fewer than seven strategies. Later, agents will be able to learn which behavior they should follow, under different circumstances. Table 6.2 lists the seven strategies.

Table 6.2. Seven Strategies for Playing the Iterated Prisoner's Dilemma

Name of Strategy	Rule for Following the Strategy
1. Nice	Always keep the bargain
2. Nasty	Always double-cross
3. Even Random	Keep the bargain 50% of the time; double-cross 50%
4. Nice Random	Keep the bargain 75% of the time; double-cross 25%
5. Tit-for-tat	On your first turn, keep the bargain; after that, do whatever the other person did last time
6. Pavlov	On your first turn, keep the bargain 75% of the time; after that, switch behaviors whenever you lose
7. Defection	Refuse to interact with the other person at all

The first two strategies are mindless, either always keeping one's bargain (Nice), or always double-crossing the other person (Nasty). The next two strategies use random numbers to model decision making, thereby producing agents that are impossible to predict precisely. Even Random has a 50 percent probability of keeping a bargain, whereas Nice Random has a 75 percent chance of keeping a bargain.

Tit-for-tat was proposed by Rapoport and was declared the winner of Axelrod's tournament. On the first exchange, it will keep its bargain. On subsequent exchanges, it will do whatever its exchange partner did last time. When interacting with a cooperative exchange partner, it will cooperate, and both will profit. Interacting with an agent following the Nice strategy, for example, it will behave exactly the same as the Nice strategy, always keeping the bargain. If it interacts with an agent following the Nasty strategy, on the first iteration it will keep the bargain, thereby allowing itself to be exploited once by the other agent. But on subsequent iterations it will double-cross, just as an agent following the Nasty strategy will. Thus, Tit-for-tat limits its vulnerability to exploitation by Nasty exchange partners, while being prepared to cooperate with nice ones.

In recent years, Pavlov (named after the early 20th-century Russian psychologist Ivan Pavlov) has joined the array of strategies frequently experimented with, and some versions of it even seem to outperform Tit-for-tat (Nowak and Sigmund 1993; Macy 1995). In our version, Pavlov starts like Nice Random, keeping the bargain 75 percent of the time. If this proves profitable, it continues to keep bargains all the time. If this stops being profitable, Pavlov switches on the next turn to double-crossing, and keeps double-crossing so long as that is profitable. Similarly, by chance, Pavlov might begin by double-crossing, and stick with this behavior so long as it is profitable. The fundamental idea of Pavlov has been described as "win-stay/lose-shift." Both Tit-for-tat and Pavlov incorporate the very simplest form of learning, because information from the past shapes present behavior.

The final strategy, Defection, is quite different. If one of the two players follows this rule, the bargain is called off, and the payoff for both players is 0.

In the following simulations, again and again the computer selects two residents of Cyburg at random. They will play the Prisoner's Dilemma 10 times. This is simply a convenient number in which the first exchange (that is, distinctive for both Tit-for-tat and Pavlov) is a small fraction of the entire series of exchanges, one-tenth to be precise. Each agent will always stick to a strategy throughout this sequence of 10 exchanges. After the first in the series of 10 exchanges, the agent will remember what happened last time, in order to have the information needed to decide what to do under both Tit-for-tat and Pavlov. Naturally, the computer will keep track of how many points each agent gains—and loses, if the total is negative.

Again, in this first simulation of the set, each of the seven groups of 6,300 Cyburg agents follows one of the seven strategies exclusively for the duration of the entire simulation. This replicates Axelrod's original tournament, which compared strategies in the abstract and did not have a clear concept of agents simulating human beings. Before we see what happens, we should consider more closely how these strategies relate to religion.

The first strategy, Nice, is equivalent to the commandment, "Thou Shalt Not Steal." We can well imagine many religious groups enshrining that principle among their highest values. The second strategy, Nasty, is the exact opposite, always double-crossing. It is hard to imagine this being a prime value of a real religious group, although it conjures up images of the legendary Thugs performing Thuggee, strangling their victims in devotion to the goddess Kali. One of the more remarkable moments in the Bible is when the Hebrews are getting ready to leave Egypt with Moses in the Exodus. They intentionally borrow valuables from their friendly Egyptian neighbors, pretending they will return them, but actually intending to run away with their neighbors' property (Exodus 12: 35–36). That's nasty! Of course, it comes some time in the Bible *before* the Ten Commandments officially outlawed stealing.

The real point of the Nasty strategy is to pose a challenge to Nice, so in the Axelrod tournament, we must give this to one of the seven groups of Cyburg residents. This will tell us what happens if there ever were a religious group that enshrined theft among its most positive values, even though we doubt that such a religious group exists today.

The two random strategies, Even Random and Nice Random, allow us to compare two groups that both may have "Thou Shalt Not Steal" among their official commandments, but which differ in their degree of adherence to this principle.

Tit-for-tat might be translated as, "Do unto others as they have done unto you." We certainly know of ancient moral codes that placed a great emphasis upon indemnity, *Wergeld*, and "an eye for an eye."

Pavlov sounds like pure expediency, "Do what works." As the name suggests, it expresses a fundamental principle of behaviorist psychology (or of economics), as Stark and I expressed it as the second axiom in *A Theory of Religion*: "Humans seek what they perceive to be rewards and avoid what they perceive to be costs" (Stark and Bainbridge 1987, 27).

Defection, refusing to play the game, could be described as the prime strategy of many well-known religious intentional communities and Anabaptist sects that withdrew into rural regions to put a distance between themselves and society, such as the Shakers, Harmony, Hutterites, and Amish (Nordhoff 1875; Hostetler and Huntington 1996; Hostetler 1993). If one or both parties to a game defects, this counts as a complete game, but the payoffs are zero, and neither Tit-for-tat nor Pavlov changes its behavior during such a nongame game.

THE FIRST CYBURG COOPERATION TOURNAMENT

We begin by dividing Cyburg residents into seven groups of exactly 6,300 members each, one for each of the seven strategies. One difference between our Cyburg tournament and some other Prisoner's Dilemma tournaments is that multiple versions of each strategy exist, namely, all the agents that play according to that strategy. For example, on a given game an agent who follows the Nasty strategy has a chance of 6,299/44,099 or just slightly less than one-seventh probability of playing with another Nasty. Table 6.3 shows results from the first simulation in this set.

This simulation ran for 44,100 games, giving each agent two chances to play a game with another agent. The most successful strategy was Nasty, earning an average 5.74 per game. Nice was least successful, losing −0.07 per game. Pavlov, a strategy that can benefit from mutual cooperation, was the second most successful, winning 3.16. A total of 408,256 bargains were kept, 46.29 percent

Table 6.3.   **Results of Playing the Prisoner's Dilemma**

Strategy	Total Points	Average Points per Game
1. Nice	−872	−0.07
2. Nasty	72,222	5.74
3. Even Random	31,399	2.47
4. Nice Random	7,987	0.64
5. Tit-for-tat	19,009	1.52
6. Pavlov	39,827	3.16
7. Defection	0	0.00

Table 6.4. "The Fall of the Roman Empire": Average Points per Game

Strategy	Inning 1	Inning 2	Inning 3	Inning 4	Inning 5	Inning 6
1. Nice	−0.13					
2. Nasty	6.70	3.76	1.57	0.53	−2.50	−10.00
3. Even Random	2.85	0.40	−1.52			
4. Nice Random	0.85	−1.33				
5. Tit-for-tat	1.61	−0.01	−1.09	−0.34		
6. Pavlov	3.74	2.04	0.77	1.19	−3.24	
Kept Bargains	62.97%	54.85%	49.65%	52.28%	35.65%	0.00%

of the total of kept bargains, double-crosses, and defections. Clearly, Defection in this context does not accomplish much, and Defection is the second-worst strategy with its preordained 0.00 payoff per game. We will drop this strategy for the time being, although defection will return in a different guise shortly.

The next experiment is what I call "The Fall of the Roman Empire," a series of games that leads progressively to disaster for the society. With Defection out of the picture, Cyburg has six groups, with exactly 7,350 members each. Except for poor Nice, these strategies are capable of double-crossing, and in this experiment they will do so with a vengeance. There will be a series of innings, each one running like the first simulation until the agents have on average played two games each. At the end of each inning, the worst strategy with a negative score will be removed from the game as having failed, and its agents will be distributed equally among the remaining strategies. Table 6.4 gives the grim results.

In the first inning of the experiment, cooperation is common, with 62.97 percent of the bargains being kept. However, agents playing the Nice strategy are outplayed by everybody except others playing Nice and those playing Tit-for-tat. The Nice strategy becomes extinct, and its 7,350 agents are distributed equally among the five remaining strategies, giving them 8,820 agents each.

In the second inning, cooperative behavior drops to 54.85 percent, and the Nice Random strategy fails. In the third inning, both Even Random and Tit-for-tat are doing very poorly, but Even Random is worse off, so it is removed. Bargain keeping has dropped just below half to 49.65 percent. In the fourth inning, with Tit-for-tat and Pavlov frequently cooperating with each other, bargain keeping rises to 52.28 percent, and Pavlov actually beats Nasty for top score. But Tit-for-tat is removed, leaving just Nasty and Pavlov, with 22,050

Table 6.5.   Stable Sets of Strategies: Average Points per Game

Strategy	Set 1	Set 2	Set 3	Set 4	Set 5	Set 6
1. Nice	0.62	7.46	4.32	6.28		2.44
2. Nasty	5.31					
3. Even Random			6.04		4.10	7.53
4. Nice Random				6.46	2.72	5.02
5. Tit-for-tat	2.14	8.16	5.34	6.98	3.77	
6. Pavlov	3.90	10.38	7.68	9.51	6.31	
Kept Bargains	64.96%	93.32%	79.18%	86.46%	71.07%	75.00%

agents each. In inning 5, both strategies drop into negative scores, and bargain keeping plunges to 35.65 percent. Nasty beats out Pavlov, but in inning 6 we see that this was a Pyrrhic victory. Once all the 44,100 agents are following the Nasty strategy, bargain keeping ceases. If this were a real society, it would become extinct at this point. As the Romans might have commented, *sic transit gloria mundi.*

Not all stories end so tragically. There are several sets of fewer than six strategies that produce a stable society, in the sense that none of the scores drop below zero. Table 6.5 shows six of them. This is not a sequence, like "The Fall of the Roman Empire," but distinct combinations of strategies that stand on their own. Interestingly, the first set includes both Nasty and Nice, showing that Nice is able to survive in an environment that contains Nasty, so long as there are a sufficient number of agents following a more or less benevolent strategy. It is worth noting that in the four that contain Pavlov but not Nasty, Pavlov does best.

REPUTATION AND REJECTION

In human affairs, some individuals often conclude that they cannot tolerate certain other individuals, and break off relations with them. Perhaps all well-established religious groups have some equivalent of excommunication or shunning. Earlier, we considered Defection as a strategy equivalent to the other six, and not a very successful one. But it may be effective as a metastrategy we can call Rejection: If interactions with a particular category of persons have been unprofitable in the past, refuse to engage in future interactions with them. This can be a powerful tool that people can use to ensure that they themselves operate in a cooperative environment, although by itself it may not increase the total level of cooperation in the society.

Table 6.6. **Individuals Rejecting Groups: Average Points per Game**

Strategy	Inning 1	Inning 2	Inning 3	Inning 5	Inning 10	Inning 20
1. Nice	0.09	0.77	1.23	2.46	4.33	5.83
2. Nasty	2.85	2.71	2.04	0.20	−5.39	−8.27
3. Even Random	1.12	1.38	1.70	1.91	1.31	0.25
4. Nice Random	0.52	0.93	1.57	2.57	4.39	5.28
5. Tit-for-tat	0.77	1.45	2.18	2.95	4.42	5.44
6. Pavlov	1.75	2.50	3.15	4.15	5.88	7.14
Kept Bargains	58.68%	51.30%	46.51%	38.72%	29.10%	22.37%

We will first consider a simulation in which individuals learn to reject categories of other individuals, and then compare what happens when the rejection occurs on the level of groups rejecting groups. Table 6.6 shows results from a simulation similar to those described above, with six strategies, and running for 20 innings. Whenever an individual has an unprofitable game with a member of a different group, that individual remembers the bad experience and refuses ever to play with a member of that group again.

The first column of figures in table 6.6 bears comparison with the first column of table 6.4. The nice strategy just barely profits from interactions in the first inning, an average of 0.09 per game, but this is better than the comparable first inning of "The Fall of the Roman Empire," in which Nice lost in the average game, −0.13. This reflects the fact that many agents following the Nice strategy got to play two or more games during the inning, and had learned to reject exchange partners from groups that had proven unprofitable in an earlier game. Perhaps even more striking, Nasty is doing more poorly now that rejection is possible, 2.85 compared with 6.70 in the first inning of "The Fall of the Roman Empire." Agents playing other strategies were learning to reject agents playing Nasty, and progressively the Nasty agents will be forced to play only with themselves, which is not a profitable game because it consists of an unrelenting series of double-crosses.

Over the 20 innings that the simulation ran, as more and more of the agents are rejecting agents from groups that often double-cross, the average profit for Nice rises, until in the 20th inning, it has reached 5.83, second only to Pavlov at 7.14. In stark contrast, Nasty has fallen below zero (which actually occurred on inning 6 when it fell to −1.03), and ends up deep into negative territory at −8.27. If we kept the simulation going until every non-Nasty agent had rejected the Nasties, the average payoff for Nasty would fall to the lowest possible −10.00.

The Even Random strategy—double-crossing half the time at random— has also been piling up rejections, and when it becomes totally isolated, its average payoff will be 0.00. Nice Random, Tit-for-tat, and Pavlov are still viable, although they have picked up some rejections and would get others if the simulation continued. After the 20th inning, still 0 percent of the other agents have learned to reject agents playing the Nice strategy. The proportions rejecting the other strategies are: Tit-for-tat = 21.36 percent, Nice Random = 30.45, Pavlov = 62.52 percent, Even Random = 79.02 percent, and Nasty = 99.52 percent.

Naturally, Tit-for-tat and Nice never reject each other, but other agents playing other strategies can have bad experiences with Tit-for-tat, because it refuses to be exploited by them. When Tit-for-tat interacts with Pavlov, and Pavlov starts by double-crossing, a terrible battle ensues. On the first turn, Pavlov profits by double-crossing Tit-for-tat, so Pavlov does the same thing on the second turn, when Tit-for-tat also double-crosses because it always does what the exchange partner did the previous time. Pavlov will then switch to keeping the bargain, having lost when both agents double-crossed each other, but Tit-for-tat will still double-cross, leading to another loss for Pavlov, who switches back to double-crossing on the next turn. In a game like this, of ten interactions, Pavlov will keep a bargain three times, and Tit-for-tat four times, with net loses of −1 and −5 points.

We can get a picture of relations between the six groups by drawing a so-ciogram, as in figure 6.1, which represents the six strategy groups by circles, and draws an arrow whenever at least 50 percent of the members of one group are willing to interact with members of the other group.

Clearly, in this sociogram Nice and Tit-for-tat win the popularity contest, followed by Nice Random, with Pavlov and Even Random getting acceptance only from Nasty, and Nasty receiving none. Three relationships fall below the 50 percent cutoff, but above 25 percent, and do not appear in the sociogram: Tit-for-Tat → Nice Random (41 percent), Even Random → Pavlov (37 percent), and Tit-for-tat → Pavlov (27 percent). Another three relationships fall below 25 percent but above 10 percent: Nice → Nice Random (23 percent), Nice → Pavlov (18 percent), and Pavlov → Even Random (17 percent).

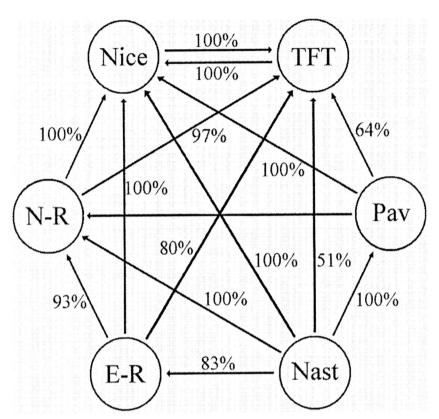

FIGURE 6.1
Sociogram of Six Strategies.

Pavlov is a fairly successful strategy, in terms of winning points in the games, but is not popular with agents playing other strategies. Nonetheless, Pavlov is capable of cooperating, as we have seen. On average, in any one game Nice has a good experience with Pavlov, but by the rule of rejection used by the simulation, even one bad experience will be traumatic and sour Nice on dealing with any member of the Pavlov group. Naturally, there is an infinite number of simulations we could do that are variations on the ones reported here, and I generally select rules that are fairly representative of the general approach, but which give clearer and somewhat speedier results.

The simulation we have just been discussing grinds along until every one of the 44,100 agents has had many, many interactions with the other groups.

While members of Nasty get rejected quickly, the others take longer. An agent playing Nice Random will eventually double-cross all 10 times—or at least enough of the 10 to discourage an agent from another group. Eventually, Nice and Tit-for-tat will be isolated in a mutual admiration society, always keeping their bargains, and the other four groups will be isolated and interacting only with members of their own group. But this takes a very long time, because each and every one of the 44,100 agents has to have sufficient experience. One factor that could speed the process of ostracism along is religion.

By promulgating a moral code, religions alert their members to what the rules are. We usually think the prime purpose is to make their members follow the rules, but another function is helping the members recognize when other individuals are crossing the line so the members can be wary. Within specific congregations, whether through formal statements in meetings or through informal gossip, members become aware of people in the community who are violating the norms. Thus, local religious groups serve a surveillance and reputation function for their members.

Another simulation was run, essentially the same as the previous one, but with a different mechanism for rejection. Whenever a member of a particular group has a bad experience with someone from another group, being repeatedly double-crossed, the member informs his denomination. Once ten or more members have sent bad notices about another group, the denomination black-balls it, and all members will henceforth reject agents who belong to it. Table 6.7 shows the very quick results of this group-rejection simulation.

The outcome is catastrophic for agents playing the Nasty strategy. They are almost immediately ostracized by the other groups, and left to gnaw on each

Table 6.7.   Groups Rejecting Groups

| | Inning 1 | | Inning 2 | |
| | | Average Points | | Average Points |
Strategy	Total Points	per Game	Total Points	per Game
1. Nice	35,551	7.26	34,570	7.35
2. Nasty	−20,505	−8.07	−19,330	−8.59
3. Even Random	272	0.11	82	0.04
4. Nice Random	11,092	4.40	10,378	4.14
5. Tit-for-tat	36,178	7.09	35,100	7.34
6. Pavlov	18,814	7.23	18,132	7.53
Kept Bargains	17.62%		16.74%	

other's bones. Even Random becomes isolated rapidly as well, in its blooming, buzzing, stochastic confusion. Nice Random survives for the time being, and to the extent it becomes isolated later on, its 75 percent rate of keeping bargains within its own community will keep it alive. Pavlov seems to be doing very well, in terms of average points per game, but it is earning far fewer points than Nice and Tit-for-tat, because it has been ostracized by other groups. Luckily for the Pavlov agents, their strategy can cooperate with itself.

Modern political sentiments tend to be offended when one group rejects another, but this is often a natural and effective self-defense mechanism that religion facilitates. Maybe some of the people who live on the wrong side of the tracks are nice, but it may be wise for a congregation to warn its members about them, if at least some of the people living over there have been known to abuse members of the congregation. Especially in societies where groups are already somewhat segregated, social mechanisms that sustain morality across denominational divides may be weak. Thus, expectations that members of a different group cannot be trusted may tragically be a self-fulfilling prophecy, but nonetheless true. Of course, this simulation may also be a metaphor for group rejection of individuals, based on bad deeds they have actually performed. In either case, a traditional function of religion may have been protecting members by establishing the good and bad reputations of people in the wider community.

REINFORCEMENT LEARNING WITH COOPERATION INCENTIVE

When Tit-for-tat won Axelrod's computer tournament 20 years ago, it was widely regarded as proof that cooperation can arise in society without such ephemeral things as values and religious faith, purely on the basis of rational self-interest. Another major piece of evidence is that many animal species cooperate, and they all seem devoid of religion (Wilson 1975). However, this does not prove that religion cannot contribute significantly to cooperation. Perhaps it does this by helping people take a long-term perspective, realizing that their own selfish interests are not best served by seeking short-term advantage—for example, through parables like the prodigal son. Perhaps, in addition, it does so by providing incentives in the form either of psychological rewards or faith-based compensators.

The final simulation of this chapter explores this by dividing Cyburg into two denominations of exactly equal size. One will be given an incentive to cooperate, whereas the other will lack this incentive and serve as a comparison group. We scrap the six strategies for playing the Prisoner's Dilemma, as well as Rejection or Defection, and utilize a reinforcement memory similar to the one belonging to the mouse in chapter 1. The following two chapters will use a vastly more complex reinforcement memory, so it is worth refreshing our own memories about the general approach here.

Each resident of Cyburg is given a brain consisting only of two real-number memory registers that can hold a number from 1 through 20. One memory register represents keeping the bargain, while the other represents double-crossing. At the beginning, they are initialized with random real numbers between 1 and 9. When preparing for an exchange, the agent calculates the sum of the two numbers, then what fraction the "keep bargain" number is of the sum. If this fraction is bigger than a random number between 1 and 0, the agent will keep the bargain. That is, the agent decides to keep the bargain with a probability proportional to the contents of the "keep bargain" memory register as a fraction of the total in both registers.

The payoffs for an exchange are the same as in the other simulations of this chapter, except that one religious group will receive an extra incentive: an additional one point for keeping the bargain (regardless of what the other agent does), and a second point for keeping the bargain if the exchange partner belongs to the same denomination. There are many ways we can incentivize these simulations, and given that this is the only simulation of this type we will examine, I wanted to illustrate the potential for subtleties. Pairs of exchange partners are drawn at random, to carry out a single exchange on a turn.

Once the exchange is finished, and the payoffs for both parties have been calculated, their memories are updated simply by adding those payoffs to the appropriate memory registers. If one agent kept the bargain, and received a positive payoff, then it will be more likely to keep the bargain in the next exchange with any agent. If the exchange was costly, however, the number on the memory register will be reduced by the amount of the negative payoff, and the agent will be less likely to cooperate next time. (Again, the numbers in each of the two memory registers are not allowed to reach 0, so there will always be some chance of selecting the associated behavior, nor is it allowed to go above 20 and dominate completely the other behavior.)

Figure 6.2 shows the average payoffs of the two groups, over 30 turns, with the experimental manipulation that agents interact only with members of

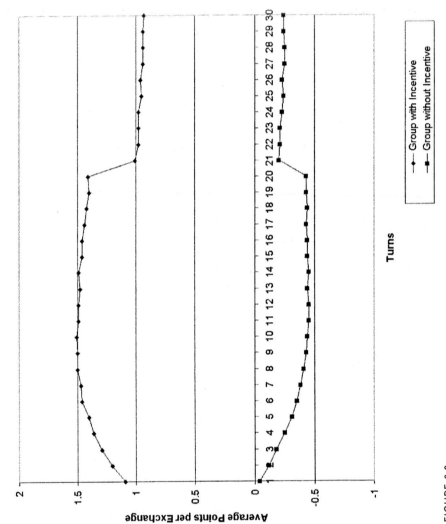

FIGURE 6.2
Effects of Incentive for Cooperation.

their own denomination for the first 20 turns, then interact at random with members of both denominations for the concluding 10 turns.

The scenario for this simulation is as follows. There are two equal-sized denominations in Cyburg, and in the recent past neither of them did much to encourage cooperation. Then some kind of revival or charismatic crusade, limited to one of the denominations, energized members' enthusiasm for cooperation. They now feel a positive spiritual boost whenever they cooperate with any human being, and with members of their own denomination they also feel an invigorating fellowship that adds to the incentive for cooperation. As in real revivals, there was an initial period in which members of the group experienced high solidarity and were unusually involved in interactions with fellow members. Then (after 20 turns) they began outreach to the other denomination, exchanging with its members half the time.

The graph shows that the denomination with the incentive for cooperation certainly does benefit. On average, they gained 1.09 points per turn, whereas the other denomination lost, getting −0.04 points per turn. A good part of the difference is accounted for by the incentive itself. But it is also true that cooperation in this group increased. By the end of the first turn, members of the incentive denomination were keeping their bargains 52.3 percent of the time, compared with only 47.8 percent of the time in the other denomination.

The graph shows that the payoff improves for several turns in the incentive group, and declines in the other. On the 20th turn, the incentive group cooperated 60.2 percent of time, compared with 28.4 percent in the other group. Then, the groups began interacting with each other half the time, and the difference in average payoff narrowed considerably. For the incentive group, part of the loss is that it gets only 1 extra point for cooperating with nonmembers, and part comes from the fact that it is now interacting with the other denomination that double-crosses more frequently. On the 30th turn, the incentive denomination is still keeping its bargains 55.75 percent of the time, compared with 24.03 percent in the nonincentive group.

SUMMATION

It is true that cooperation can emerge in society without religion, and even with religion we know that cooperation is imperfect. However, this chapter has suggested ways in which religion might facilitate cooperation: (1) by promulgating potentially cooperative interaction strategies that benefit members,

(2) by improving the efficiency of reputation-based rejection of bad exchange partners, and (3) by providing direct incentives for cooperation.

The simulation we called "The Fall of the Roman Empire" points out that a set of conditions may become established in a society that progressively erodes cooperation, leading ultimately to disastrous disintegration of the entire society, until it can no longer sustain human life. If religion significantly strengthens cooperation, then secularization threatens the very well-being of society.

Although our research in this area is not sufficiently developed yet to be sure where the truth lies, these simulations raise the issue of moral consensus. This returns us to the sociological debate about whether religious monopoly leads to more or to less religious mobilization of the population. If there are many competing religions, with distinctly different moral codes, does their diversity erode morality in general? Perhaps we must leave this question for empirical research in the real world.

7

Faith

Previous chapters have simulated humans acting in a context where religion already exists. Now we are ready to simulate the birth of faith itself. This requires new modules in the computer program, but in fact the memory registers we will use to store religious belief include the same ones we used in chapter 5, and they are arranged in a structure inspired by that possessed by the simulated mouse in chapter 1, but merely assembling more bytes of memory. In this chapter and the next, we will use various metaphors to encode human belief into the software, but they have two strong points of origin. First, the artificial intelligence system will not only originate religious faith, but it will do so in the same way that it endows the agents with the ability to learn how to gain material rewards, thus proving the competence of the AI. Second, the motivating concepts all come from the quarter-century of theoretical work I have had the privilege of doing in collaboration with Rodney Stark and others, so the connection to social and cognitive theory is direct.

THE THEORY OF RELIGION

In a series of coauthored publications (Stark and Bainbridge 1980b, 1985, 1987; Bainbridge and Stark 1984) building on work each had done before collaborating (Glock and Stark 1965; Bainbridge 1978), Stark and I have offered a comprehensive theory of religion. The key publication is our 1987 book *A Theory of Religion,* which outlines how 344 propositions (theorems) about human behavior might be derived from a set of seven axioms assisted by 104 definitions. Here we have space only to hint at the direction the theory takes, and I have listed here the axioms plus a few important propositions and associated definitions.

Axioms and Selected Propositions of a Theory of Religion

The Axioms:

Axiom 1: Human perception and action take place through time, from the
past into the future.

Axiom 2: Humans seek what they perceive to be rewards and avoid what
they perceive to be costs.

Axiom 3: Rewards vary in kind, value, and generality.

Axiom 4: Human action is directed by a complex but finite information-
processing system that functions to identify problems and
attempt solutions to them.

Axiom 5: Some desired rewards are limited in supply, including some that
simply do not exist.

Axiom 6: Most rewards sought by humans are destroyed when they are
used.

Axiom 7: Individual and social attributes that determine power are
unequally distributed among persons and groups in any society.

Selected Propositions and Definitions:

Proposition 3: In solving problems, the human mind must seek
explanations.

Definition 7: The mind is the set of human functions that directs the action
of a person.

Definition 10: Explanations are statements about how and why rewards
may be obtained and costs are incurred.

Proposition 4: Explanations are rewards of some level of generality.

Proposition 6: In pursuit of desired rewards, humans will exchange rewards
with other humans.

Proposition 14: In the absence of a desired reward, explanations often will
be accepted which posit attainment of the reward in the
distant future of in some other nonverifiable context.

Definition 18: Compensators are postulations of reward according to
explanations that are not readily susceptible to unambiguous
evaluation.

Proposition 22: The most general compensators can be supported only by
supernatural explanations.

Definition 20: Compensators that substitute for a cluster of many rewards
and for rewards of great scope are called general
compensators.

Definition 22: Religion refers to systems of general compensators based on
supernatural assumptions.

While not denying the possibility of God's existence, our theory attempts to explain human religious behavior without assuming the truth of religion. Therefore, there is no axiom asserting the existence of the supernatural. Legend has it that the great French astronomer and mathematician Pierre Simon de Laplace, when asked by Napoleon why his theories said nothing about God, replied, "I have no need of that hypothesis" (de Morgan 1956). Nor does our theory.

Because they possess complex information-processing systems (minds), humans are able to frame *explanations* (or, as I personally prefer to call them, *algorithms*; cf. Bainbridge 2003), which are statements about how and why rewards may be obtained and costs are incurred. Good explanations are valuable because they permit a person to obtain rewards. Thus, explanations are instrumental rewards, comparable to the material resources that are often needed to obtain a desired reward. Humans seek explanations because they are valuable. Like many other rewards, explanations can often be obtained best through the aid of other human beings, typically through processes of social exchange.

Rewards vary in their generality. Therefore, explanations can be more or less general. A specific explanation tells a person how to obtain a very specific reward under narrowly defined circumstances. A general explanation covers a variety of specific means for obtaining a wide range of rewards.

Tragically, many of the rewards humans seek are very difficult to obtain. Some may not exist at all. The example we have used most often is eternal life. This is a very general reward, and perhaps the most valuable one, because it permits a person to obtain a variety of more specific rewards. Other things being equal, the more general and valuable a reward, the more difficult it is to obtain. If a reward is hard to get, explanations about how to obtain it may be very difficult to evaluate. Therefore, people in pursuit of very general and valuable rewards often must take explanations on faith from other people who offer them.

Compensators are postulations of reward according to explanations that are not readily susceptible to unambiguous evaluation. Compensators are treated by humans as if they were rewards, and they vary according to the generality, value, and kinds of rewards for which they substitute. One very general compensator is belief in an afterlife. Short of dying, it is hard to test the existence of heaven.

Religions are systems of general compensators based on supernatural assumptions. The word *supernatural* refers to forces beyond or outside nature that can suspend, alter, or ignore physical forces. Steven Pinker (1997, 556), director of the Center for Cognitive Neuroscience at the Massachusetts Institute of Technology, has argued that people form their image of the supernatural by taking concepts from the natural world and altering them only slightly. Thus, a god is conceptualized as a person—with senses, cognition, desire, speech, and behavior—but vastly more powerful than an ordinary human being. Thus, a god is the ideal exchange partner.

Our theory book examines in detail how the exchange of explanations and other rewards among humans can gradually create beliefs in supernatural beings who are thought to provide the rewards that are difficult or impossible to obtain from other human beings. But as our book went to press, we were far from satisfied that we had conclusively derived our many propositions; rather, we had sketched the outlines of such derivations, remaining rather vague on the means to complete them. A key point is that humans learn to seek exchange partners from whom to obtain rewards and, further, they learn to accept the advice of trusted exchange partners concerning the identities of other good potential exchange partners. The challenge, then, was to write these ideas into a computer program.

A MARTIAN SCENARIO

There is much to be said in favor of simple simulation programs modeling just a few propositions about social life. They are easier to write, debug, and explain. They permit unconfused examination of just those concepts the social theorist wishes to analyze, and they facilitate accurate interpretation of unexpected results. But for two reasons, we shall consider in our pair of concluding chapters an especially ornate simulation program and scenario.

First, the theory of religion derives supernaturally oriented social behavior from nonreligious behavior, seeing religion as an inevitable but secondary result of exchanges undertaken to gain economic and affective rewards. Therefore, a fairly complex society must be postulated before religion can emerge.

Second, the sociology of religion has not previously employed simulations and thus is unfamiliar with the wide range of possibilities they offer. Therefore, the verisimilitudes of an ornate program that models many theoretically nonessential features of real human life have heuristic functions.

To give the scenario coherence, and to attach clear metaphors to the simulation's features, we will imagine that Cyburg is a self-sustaining community on the planet Mars. Utopian literature, which can be seen in part as qualitative literary simulation of alternative social facts, has often used fables about Mars to illustrate and develop its themes. For example, Kurd Lasswitz in 1897 and H. G. Wells in 1898 both postulated Martian societies technically far advanced over those on Earth, and considered what that superiority would imply about their moral development. For Lasswitz, a Kantian scholar, scientific superiority meant moral superiority as well, while for Wells, a critic of progress, it meant savage immorality.

Other authors, notably Ray Bradbury (1950) and Kim Stanley Robinson (1993, 1994, 1996), have used Mars to analyze terrestrial psychological complexes and social issues. A whole shelf of novels used Martian societies as vehicles for religious debate—for example, Edgar Rice Burroughs in 1918, C. S. Lewis in 1938, and Robert Heinlein in 1961.

We have long known that the actual colonization of Mars is physically possible, if economically challenging (von Braun 1953; Carr 1981; Cooper 1981; McKay 1982; Zubrin 1996), so there is nothing unconventional about this scenario. One of its advantages is that it allows us to write a series of simulations using the same scenario, describing the development of a society from scratch, including the gradual creation of a distinctive culture.

The unmanned Viking landers that analyzed the Martian soil in 1976 were eventually followed by stalwart robot heroes Pathfinder, Spirit, and Opportunity, which could actually move across the surface of the planet and explore the territory. Let us imagine that through a Herculean effort, the nations of the Earth have cooperated to establish a Martian settlement of 44,100 residents. For the first time we will be able to model fertility and cultural transmission to a new generation. Thus, we will imagine that the colonists include 22,050 men and 22,050 women.

The community will need electricity to run its machines and chemical processing devices, so 11,025 small solar energy plants have been set up, each the property of one of the colonists who operates it and is prepared to exchange energy for other rewards with colonists having other resources. Another 11,025 colonists operate mines that take energy and use it to dig up and melt ice to make water, a second essential resource. There are also 11,025 hydroponic farms that require only water to grow food in the Martian soil under Plexiglas domes. Finally, there are 11,025 oxygen factories, each owned and operated by a colonist, manufacturing oxygen to breathe through electrolysis of water, using electricity and water acquired through exchanges with colonists operating energy plants and ice mines.

Periodically (Axiom 1), each colonist consumes some of each of these four rewards, for example, eating food and thereby depleting his or her supply of it (Axiom 6). A colonist who runs completely out of a consumable will die, and so colonists are motivated to increase their store of the reward they have least of, even at the cost of giving up some of a reward they have in relative surplus. Thus, at any given moment, colonists vary in how much they value one unit of different rewards and thus are able to conduct mutually rewarding exchanges (Axiom 2, Axiom 3).

Colonists remember something about the people who have proven good suppliers of a reward in the past, and will tend to return to similar people when next they desire the same reward (Axiom 4, Axiom 2). Each of the factory operators can make a profit, because, for example, 2 units of water can be produced at the cost of 1 unit of energy. After a successful exchange, the two parties may have a chat, each providing the other with information about other people who have proven to be a good source for a reward in the past.

Notice that this fictional economy models the essentials of much more complex systems of exchange. Those possessing energy plants are like a capitalist class, since the mere ownership of their properties gives them a steady income of valuable electric power. They do not need to give away other resources in exchanges in order to prosper, so they are likely to become rich. Operators of water, food, and oxygen facilities can become prosperous, but because they must give away half of their product to get the supplies to make it, they are in a lower class than the energy barons.

As the simulation runs, the colonists get many sequential turns (Axiom 1) in which each can contact another colonist and propose a trade, offering a certain amount of the supply he or she has most of in return for an identical amount of the supply he or she has least of. If the colonist to whom the trade is offered would also benefit, the exchange takes place (Axiom 2). Thus, the colonists are continually producing new resources, winding up individually with surpluses of one economic reward, and exchanging to even out their stocks of all four economic rewards. In so doing, they create an economy that successfully distributes the four rewards, permitting survival and continued production.

This very simple economic system incorporates a structure of rewards, some of which are instrumental in producing other rewards, each being a consumable necessity of life (Axiom 3). Energy, water, food, and oxygen are commercial rewards that can be cashed out in terms of each other. But not all rewards humans seek are tangible or can be cashed out in terms of material rewards (Axiom 3).

Martians seek romantic love, once a basic supply of material goods has been assured. For a while after an erotic encounter, a colonist is little interested in sex, but if other needs have been satisfied, and time has turned satiation to lust, each will seek a lover of the opposite sex. If one is found, intercourse will take place.

As on Earth, on Mars sex makes babies. Not every romantic episode produces a child, but if the colony has room for one more person—because somebody has died, leaving open a vacancy—one will be born. The parents teach their child some of what they know about life, giving it information about the kinds of colonists who have proven good exchange partners in the past (Axiom 4). Babies quickly grow up in the weak Martian gravity, and take their places in the economic system.

The parents gradually reach old age and begin to die. As they do so, children and grandchildren are born to take their places. Thus, over a single run of the simulation, several tens of thousands of people may be born, live, and die, although there are never more than 44,100 agents in Cyburg at any given time.

As they get older, Martians worry more and more about approaching death. They seek an exchange partner who could provide them with extension of life. Unfortunately, the humans do not have the power to save their fellow colonists from death by old age (Axiom 5), but many of them come to believe in gods they think can grant eternal life. Some people hope the gods can provide them love or material rewards, as well as life, and many of the features of religion arise on Mars.

THE MASTER MIND OF MARS

In order to handle this complex social environment, the Cyburg agents require rather complex minds. The 44,100 people know that they are divided among a number of groups—whether two, three, or four, they do not know—and that particular rewards can be gotten most readily from some groups, but they do not initially know which ones. Each person enters into a number of exchanges with people chosen at random, seeking whatever rewards he or she most needs. For each reward, the person gradually develops a theory about how many groups there are and which group is the best source of the reward. Thus, each person's mind is represented by six direct reinforcement neural nets, one for each reward. The neural net is capable of comparing the effectiveness of different categorization schemes, as well as applying the schemes to find the best exchange partners.

If we had a huge computer, teams of professional programmers, and all the time in the world, we could create a very realistic simulation. People would learn to recognize faces and other visual cues. "This is Bob. He wears a baker's uniform. When I ask him for food, he gives me some. I must remember to look for Bob when I need food. If I can't find Bob, somebody else in a baker's uniform might do." At the present level of computer development, this would be quite difficult, although just barely possible, and also superfluous for exploring abstract theories. We can stipulate that people have the means to recognize each other and place each other in categories, relying upon a simple mathematical system to do this in a theoretically satisfactory if not superficially realistic way.

I encoded individual identity and group membership into ID numbers, for the 44,100 residents of Cyburg: 1 through 44,100. At the beginning of a run, the experimenter can decide how many groups there should be (2, 3, or 4) and which groups should produce the various rewards (except eternal life, which no one has, and sex, which distinguishes even ID numbers from odd ones). If there are two groups, then one group consists of all the odd numbers and the other group consists of the even numbers. If there are three, then the computer counts off every third number into a group; if four groups, every fourth number. The simulated people do not know how many groups there actually are nor which groups are the best sources of particular rewards, but as they interact with each other, they analyze the ID numbers to develop theories about the system in which they find themselves.

There are three mental steps each person takes in each turn of the simulation. First, the person decides which reward to seek. Each has a certain amount of each reward, and selects the one in shortest supply. As time passes, the individuals consume rewards as a part of living (drinking water, for example) and working (an oxygen producer needs water from which to derive the oxygen, and energy with which to extract it). In a successful exchange, people give something they value less than the thing they get, and a shortage of any particular reward impels them to seek an exchange partner who can give it to them.

Second, they decide which theory about Cyburg's social groups to follow in selecting an exchange partner from whom to see the reward. That is, how many groups are there? The simulation program was written to allow the agents to imagine as many as 5 groups, but here we will limit them to 4. Thus, the agent must decide whether to act upon the assumption there are 2 groups, 3 groups, or 4 groups.

Third, which specific group should the exchange partner belong to? I specifically set up the three decisions so that they are largely separate. This has an important meaning. The agents do not have fully consistent theories of the nature of the world they live in, just as humans do not have a fully consistent theory of their world.

Stark and I analyzed this issue in our theoretical treatise under the headings of "Culture and Society" and "Social and Cultural Development" (Stark and Bainbridge 1987, 60–77). These are two of the sections of the work that illustrate most vividly that our perspective is cognitive, rather than behaviorist. Throughout life, each individual discovers a very large number of brute facts about the environment; much of this learning is motivated by the search for rewards and the attempt to avoid costs. As individuals, we learn to make generalizations: dogs bite, ice cream tastes good, four is bigger than two. Through speech and example, we share information with each other and it accumulates, but both individually and collectively we have great difficulty framing general rules (explanations, algorithms). Some of the pertinent propositions and definitions from this part of our analysis are listed here.

Selected Propositions and Definitions about Cultural Systems

Proposition 35: Human culture occurs through the accumulation and transmission of explanations over time.

Definition 30: *Culture* is the total complex of explanation exchanged by humans.

Proposition 36: The explanations of a religion are a cultural system.

Definition 31: Explanations form a *cultural system* if they are part of a greater explanation that includes them.

Proposition 37: A culture is created by a society and consists of whatever
explanations are accepted by the members of that society.
Proposition 38: Social cleavages tend to produce cultural cleavages.
Proposition 39: Any culture contains a number of cultural systems.
Proposition 40: Humans retain the culture that appears most rewarding.
Proposition 45: The more complex the culture, the greater the degree of
cultural specialization.
Definition 33: *Cultural specialization* refers to the tendency of individuals to
master parts of their culture and to engage in exchanges with
others who have mastered different parts.
Proposition 47: Cultural specialties evolve into cultural systems, dependent
upon the discovery of explanations that prove valuable in
uniting the relevant subexplanations.

In the next chapter we will come back to the subject of culture, but notice
that the same logic applies to individual cognition: Knowledge of miscellaneous
facts about some sphere of life evolves into cognitive systems, dependent upon
the discovery of explanations that prove valuable in uniting the relevant subexplanations. But it is quite difficult to find those general explanations that can
bring together many lesser explanations, thereby giving humans great power
to make good decisions. This is one of the reasons that human perception,
decision making, and action are suboptimal. We have many separate mental
models of different parts of the world. Most of them work pretty well, but far
from perfectly, and we often have difficulty seeing how they fit together.

The agents that inhabit Cyburg have the capacity to learn how many groups
of agents there are, and they can learn which group among a set is the right one
to seek for a particular reward. But they cannot look at the entire system from
outside and see its true nature. They are forced to stumble by trial and error,
frequently sticking with suboptimal solutions to problems, and they are not
fully logical in how they fit data together. The very fact that they are capable of
learning implies they are not born with the truth, and probably dooms them
never quite to achieve it.

The computer memory that does this learning is organized as rectangular
blocks of cells, each containing a weight. Here, we have limited the agents to
conceptualizing no more than 4 groups, so for one reward the matrix consists of
12 memory cells, in a 3-by-4 configuration, with 3 other cells set aside to store
variance calculations I will explain momentarily. That is a total of 15 memory

Table 7.1. The Initial Contents of the Energy Registers of One Agent

	Group #0	Group #1	Group #2	Group #3
2 Groups	732	673	554	709
3 Groups	628	967	938	561
4 Groups	941	534	728	566

registers for each reward, each capable of holding a large or high-precision real number, or a total of 90 for all 6 rewards. Of course, across all 44,100 agents, that is a total of 3,969,000 double-precision real numbers, taking up nearly 32 megabytes of the computer's memory.

At the beginning of the simulation, the computer initializes the matrix by putting random numbers in the cells. This is not merely a computer house-keeping chore because it represents the fact that the units in any nervous system have a more or less random bias that they may overcome through learning but which predisposes the system to act in certain ways initially. For the simulations here, those random numbers ranged between 500 and 999. Table 7.1 shows the numbers that happened to be in the energy registers for an agent who makes water, and thus will have to learn where to seek energy to make it with. Later, we will explain why we name the groups starting with zero: Group #0, Group #1, Group #2, Group #3.

When it is time for this agent to seek another agent who might be able to provide energy, the agent must select a theory about how many groups there are: 2, 3, or 4. The agent does this by looking at the variances of the numbers in each row of table 7.1. Variance, as the name hints, is a measure of variability. It measures how dispersed the numbers are from their mean—how far they are on average from their average. To be more precise, it is the average of the squared deviations of the numbers from their arithmetic mean. Notice the numbers in the first row of table 7.1: 732, 673, 554, and 709. Their variance (allowing for rounding error) is 4,698. If these numbers were all identical, the variance would be zero.

As the simulation progresses, these numbers will come to represent how much reward the agent has gotten for acting on the assumption that the par-ticular cell represents the true number of groups, and which group is the best source of energy. Therefore, a good solution will mean a row of num-bers that are very different from each other, thus with a high variance. The variance would be high, because the theory represented by the row of figures

Table 7.2.   Variances across Theories of Groups

	Raw Variance	Variance as Proportion
2 Groups	4,698	7.41%
3 Groups	32,639	51.51%
4 Groups	26,026	41.07%

does a good job of distinguishing rewarding from unrewarding sources of energy.

Table 7.2 shows the variances for the three rows of table 7.1, along with their proportions of the total variance. The sum of the three variances is 4,698 + 32,639 + 26,026 = 63,363. For example, 4,698 is about 7.41 percent of 63,363. When the agent has to decide which of the three theories to follow (2 groups, 3 groups, 4 groups), it will have a probability of selecting each of these rows represented by its proportion of the variance. Thus, it is more likely to select the row (or theory) that distinguishes rewarding from nonrewarding sources.

The most likely choice, given the numbers in tables 7.1 and 7.2, is for the agent to assume there are 3 groups, because this theory has a variance of 51.51 percent. Let's say the agent does make that choice for its first move. Then it has to decide which group to seek the exchange partner from. Table 7.3 expresses the same data as table 7.1, but as percentages of the total in each row. That is, if the agent decides there are three groups, it has a 20.3 percent chance of deciding energy should be sought from Group #0, and a 31.25 percent chance of going for Group #1.

Another way of looking at the contents of the agent's memory, which we will find better for comparison later, is in terms of the total probabilities in table 7.4. Again, we are looking at the same data, but in a different way. The variance numbers are the same as in table 7.2, but now we are expressing the other cells in terms of total probability of selecting that cell. If there is a 51.51 percent chance of selecting 3 groups, and within that selection a

Table 7.3.   Probabilities within Each Theory

	Group #0 (%)	Group #1 (%)	Group #2 (%)	Group #3 (%)	Total (%)
2 Groups	27.44	25.22	20.76	26.57	100.00
3 Groups	20.30	31.25	30.32	18.13	100.00
4 Groups	33.98	19.28	26.29	20.44	100.00

Table 7.4. Initial Probabilities of Decision: Agent Seeking Energy

	Variance (%)	Group #0 (%)	Group #1 (%)	Group #2 (%)	Group #3 (%)
2 Groups	7.41	2.03	1.87	1.54	1.97
3 Groups	51.51	10.46	16.10	15.62	9.34
4 Groups	41.07	13.96	7.92	10.80	8.40

20.3 percent chance of selecting Group #0, then we multiply these numbers to get the overall probability of deciding "there are three groups and Group #0 is the right one": $0.5151 \times 0.2030 = 0.1046$, or 10.46 percent. The percentages in the 12 cells (other than the 3 variance cells) total 100 percent. Technically, we can call this system a *hierarchical, variance-maximizing network*.

Once the agent has made a decision, it seeks an exchange partner from the selected group. If the exchange goes well, the agent will receive up to 250 units of energy. Here is how that affects learning: The computer will add those 250 units to the contents of the appropriate memory cell. Indeed, although the agent selected one theory only, of the three available, the information gain applies to all three theories, so the 250 is added to the one appropriate cell in each of the three rows. If the exchange partner is unable or unwilling to provide energy, then 100 is subtracted from each of those cells (but each cell will not go below 50). This is called *direct reinforcement*, because the payoff is going directly into the memory register, unlike the more indirect *back propagation* method used for chapter 5.

Over a series of exchanges, with luck the numbers will increase in some memory registers, and decrease in others, representing the agent learning a profitable theory about what kinds of exchange partners there are, and which kinds are a good source of energy. Table 7.5 shows the pattern in the particular agent's energy memory registers after a lifetime (maximum 1,000 turns) of seeking energy. The first thing to notice is how vastly different the numbers are from those in table 7.4, demonstrating how much the agent has learned during its lifetime. Now, the agent thinks there are probably only 2 groups

Table 7.5. Final Probabilities of Decision: Agent Seeking Energy

	Variance (%)	Group #0 (%)	Group #1 (%)	Group #2 (%)	Group #3 (%)
2 Groups	64.04	62.77	0.14	0.50	0.63
3 Groups	7.14	2.38	2.39	2.31	0.06
4 Groups	28.83	19.96	0.02	8.63	0.22

in Cyburg (variance = 64.04 percent), with some real possibility there are 4 groups (variance = 28.83 percent). This agent has little credence in the idea there are 3 groups (variance = 7.14 percent). Assuming there are 2 groups, the agent is quite sure Group #0 is the one to seek energy from (62.77 percent), but on the assumption there might be 4 groups, then Group #0 is moderately likely (19.6 percent), but Group #2 has some chance too (8.63 percent).

The truth is, there are actually 4 groups, and agents in Group #0 are the energy producers. The agent whose mind we see in table 7.5 will never know the truth, just as we humans will never know the full truth about our own lives and universe. This agent labors under the technically false belief that there are probably only 2 groups. However, this is not a bad theory, because it excludes half the population of Cyburg. The agent correctly knows that they are *not* energy producers. Thus, again, we see an illustration of the principle that learning optimizes but is never optimal.

Another important principle that this kind of memory was designed to illustrate, like that of the stupid mouse in chapter 1, is that human beings never have absolute conviction about anything. Even when faith is strong, there are doubts. In this case, the agent is only about twice as confident there are 2 groups rather than 4. There is always hope that any conceivable thing might possibly be true.

As a final step in grasping how the memory works, let us look into the mind of a different agent, one who makes oxygen. To make oxygen, one needs both energy and water, so table 7.6 shows the end-of-simulation contents of this agent's energy and water memories. This oxygen producer thinks that with respect to energy there could be 2 groups (variance = 46.36 percent), or there

Table 7.6. Oxygen-Making Agent Seeking Both Energy and Water

	Variance (%)	Group #0 (%)	Group #1 (%)	Group #2 (%)	Group #3 (%)
ENERGY:					
2 Groups	46.36	44.57	0.05	0.85	0.89
3 Groups	4.73	1.49	1.60	1.55	0.09
4 Groups	48.91	48.61	0.18	0.05	0.05
WATER:					
2 Groups	46.88	0.06	45.40	0.71	0.72
3 Groups	5.07	1.73	1.44	1.81	0.08
4 Groups	48.05	0.26	47.47	0.06	0.26

might be 4 groups (48.91 percent), but there are very unlikely to be 3 groups (4.73 percent). And with respect to water, this agent is again about equally split between 2 groups (variance = 46.88 percent) and 4 groups (48.05 percent). Thus, this agent really does not have a comprehensive theory about how many groups there are, but the agent's experience seeking two different rewards gives it very similar feelings on this issue. Within each theory about how many groups there are, the agent is quite convinced that energy can best be gotten from members of Group #0 (44.57 + 48.61 = 93.18 percent), and that water can best be gotten from members of Group #1 (92.87 percent), which is actually quite right. This agent lacks full knowledge of its environment, but within that environment it has done a very good job of mastering economic exchange for the two resources it especially needs to do its job.

If the agents were really wise and understood their economy fully, they would notice that real energy producers are not necessarily the only people they can get energy from. The four groups are Group #0 = energy, Group #1 = water, Group #2 = food, Group #3 = oxygen. Both Groups #1 and #3 need extra energy to run their business, whereas Group #2 does not, needing only water to make food. Thus, sometimes agents in Group #2 might be willing to give up some surplus energy they just happen to have. This would give the false impression that both Groups #0 and #2 were good sources of energy, or rather that there are only 2 groups, mentally combining Group #0 and Group #2. A second reason the theory of 2 groups might be favored is because it offers a simple model of the world they dwell in. Like humans and the agents we saw in chapter 5, these agents have a bias for simplicity, which sometimes leads them into error.

FAITH IN THE GODS

As the simulation runs, the agents slowly consume resources. A water producer uses up 250 units of energy to make 500 units of water. A food producer uses up 250 units of water to make 500 units of food. An oxygen producer uses up 125 units of energy and 125 units of water to make 500 units of oxygen. The lucky energy producers manufacture 500 units of energy at no cost in other resources. But on each turn, each agent consumes 1 unit of each of the 4 resources, just to live, and also consumes 1 unit of life itself. If the agents can do their work well, and develop satisfactory theories of exchange partners, they can replenish the energy, water, food, and oxygen they use up. But they cannot replenish life. This does not prevent them from seeking it, however.

Whenever a given agent has a turn, it inspects its resources (energy, water, food, oxygen, and life) to see which is lowest. Then it uses the part of its memory devoted to that reward to decide what kind of exchange partner to seek. The procedures are identical for life as for the other four rewards. But because humans cannot give each other extended life, the outcome is slightly different. If the agent selects life, seeks an exchange partner following a particular theory, and actually interacts with a human being, the result will be a loss of 100 points in the memory registers that identify the exchange partner. That happens for the other reward, as well, if the exchange partner cannot provide them, but it always happens for life. Thus, as the simulation progresses, the agent will lose faith that other agents who actually exist within the system can provide life.

The rectangular memory system allows the agent to imagine three categories of persons that do not actually exist:

- Members of the third group, when there are two groups
- Members of the fourth group, when there are two groups
- Members of the fourth group, when there are three groups

These concepts seem logically inconsistent, to say the least! But where is the logical consistency in saying that God exists but is not part of the natural world? Where is the logical consistency in saying that God has a mind, but no brain? Intelligence is the evolutionary result of a billion generations of animals seeking rewards and avoiding costs in a material world, and it is based in cells called neurons in the brain. Today, intelligence can also be embodied in computer chips, but they are no less material than neurons. So what neural units comprise the mind of God? Where is the consistency in saying that science cannot evaluate the existence of God, when science is merely the rigorous formulation of all the methods humans possess for understanding everything that is real?

More formally, the categorization process used by Cyburg's agents can be translated into modulo arithmetic. Computer programming languages typically have an operator that reports the integer remainder from dividing one number by another. In BASIC and Pascal, it is called *mod*, while dialects of the C language confusingly use "%" for the same operator. This is why I numbered the four groups of agents 0, 1, 2, and 3. These are the integer remainders after dividing an agent's ID number (1 through 44,100) by 4.

In categorizing potential exchange partners, the simulated people employ modulo arithmetic to decode the ID numbers of other people. For example, if one is using a two-group system of categorization, a person with ID number 5 is in Group #5 mod 2, or Group #1. With a three-group system, person number 5 is in Group #2 because 5 mod 3 = 2. In this case, four groups give the same result as two groups, because 5 mod 4 = 1.

Our simulated people depart from conventional modulo arithmetic because they are able to imagine a number i such that i mod j is equal to or greater than j. That is, they can imagine i such that i mod 2 = 3. In conventional modulo arithmetic, this is impossible. Mathematics categorizes numbers in many different ways, for example: real numbers, irrational numbers, imaginary numbers, and natural numbers (positive integers). I use the term *supernatural number* for an integer i such that i mod $j \geq j$ for some positive integer, j.

Nonsense, one might say. However, Oswald Spengler (1926, vol. I, 53–90) argued that different cultures have different mathematics (in the plural), and writers in the "strong programme" tradition in the sociology of science (Watson 1990; Bloor 1991) report that other societies have systems of number that are profoundly different from our own. In any case, the whole point of the present exercise is to develop a way of modeling human belief in supernatural beings that are somehow like humans—at least, in that people can imagine them as exchange partners—but beings that do not exist within the same natural world as the believers. Supernatural numbers are the ID numbers of gods. Revelation 13:18 in the Bible tells us that the number of the Beast is 666; perhaps the number of God is i, such that i mod 2 = 2. An atheist would argue that here i mod 2 = 0, and the belief that "i mod 2 = 2" is a mere superstition.

Supernatural numbers can be manipulated like natural numbers in many ways, and my computer programs run without crashing or producing obviously garbage output. For example, memory registers can easily be addressed for interactions with an exchange partner named by a given supernatural number. But an exchange with that supernatural partner cannot be completed within the world of the simulated people. This means that the agents cannot conclusively reject the hypothesis that one of these supernatural beings could provide eternal life.

Table 7.7.   Two Agents Seeking Eternal Life

	Variance (%)	Group #0 (%)	Group #1 (%)	Group #2 (%)	Group #3 (%)
WATER AGENT:					
2 Groups	56.57	1.70	1.70	33.45	19.72
3 Groups	37.23	1.34	1.34	12.92	21.63
4 Groups	6.20	0.92	2.87	1.25	1.16
ENERGY AGENT:					
2 Groups	62.67	2.16	2.16	33.75	24.60
3 Groups	37.33	2.41	2.41	2.41	30.10
4 Groups	0.00	0.00	0.00	0.00	0.00

Table 7.7 shows the theories of how to get life, held by two agents at the end of the simulation described above. The first is the water-producing agent we first examined, and the second is one of the wealthy energy-producing agents. In both cases, the agents believe that the three kinds of supernatural agents are the most likely sources of life. We can easily quantify the strength of their convictions by summing up the percentages for the three supernatural categories: Group #3 of 2, Group #4 of 2, Group #4 of 3. About 74.8 percent of the time, the water-producing agent would seek life from a supernatural being, and the percentage is 88.15 for the energy-producing agent. Over the 1,000 turns, the average for all the agents rose from 25.22 percent to 79.33 percent.

The difference between the two agents is theoretically meaningful. Notice that the rich energy-producer has absolutely no faith in a theory that postulates 4 groups for eternal life, whereas the water producer retains some slight hope. Recall that the theory there are 4 groups of agents in the simulation is the ultimate truth, which we know but the agents do not, and none of them can provide eternal life. Energy producers are rich not only in the sense they wind up with more resources but also they do not have to work—to engage in exchanges to obtain needed raw materials for their production. They do engage in exchanges for the necessities of life, but they have the financial leverage to obtain them fairly easily. Thus they have simply more time to be seeking eternal life, and therefore become more knowledgeable from a greater number of learning experiences. So to speak, the theology of the elite is more refined than the theology of the masses. This is not only realistic but also dovetails with some simulation results we will offer in the concluding chapter, when we compare the religious beliefs of three social classes: upper, middle, and lower.

SUMMATION

The standard theory of religious faith, as presented here, is a theory of cognitive error, like Allport's theory of prejudice mentioned in chapter 5. The prevailing etiquette in the social science of religion frowns upon any suggestion that religious beliefs are false, perhaps because the majority of social scientists of religion are themselves religious, and their relatively few irreligious colleagues value politeness. At one point in the introduction to our theoretical treatise, Stark and I acknowledged that "work such as ours is potentially inimical to faith" (Stark and Bainbridge 1987, 23), but we probably should have italicized the word *potentially*. There is nothing shameful about the fact that religious faith depends in large measure upon cognitive error, because cognitive error is endemic in all areas of human thought.

Evolution has blessed humans with brains that are just barely able to cope with the challenges of life. About as soon as civilization could evolve, it did, so *Homo sapiens* found itself civilized long before it could evolve really capable minds. The practical consequences of this incongruity are all around us.

I find it singularly amazing that most humans in modern societies can read and write. What evolutionary pressures on the East African savannah, millennia ago, could have possibly have predisposed us for literacy? Three of my own most immediate relatives were dyslexic, and I myself had the greatest difficulty learning spelling and never did master penmanship—but the miracle is that anybody can express and perceive complex meanings through tiny marks on a page. As millions of students can testify, learning mathematics is a highly unnatural act. Evolution did not design us to be scientists, although apparently we can transfer skills from more practical activities and thus were able (painfully enough) to create science over the centuries.

Instead of error, one could say that the standard theory of religion concerns uncertainty, indeterminacy, and extrapolation from the known into the unknown toward the unknowable. The central concept of compensators was prepared by the following three propositions about the limits of knowledge (Stark and Bainbridge 1987, 35):

P11 It is impossible to know for certain that a given reward does not exist.

P12 When a desired reward is relatively unavailable, explanations that promise to provide it are costly and difficult to evaluate correctly.

P13 The more valued or general a reward, the more difficult will be valuations of explanations about how to obtain it.

In a much later part of the argument, we distinguished magic from religion and noted (Stark and Bainbridge 1987, 105):

P91   Magic is more vulnerable than religion to disconfirmation.

Def.52 *Magic* refers to specific compensators that promise to provide desired rewards without regard for evidence concerning the designated means.

By dealing primarily with general compensators and with supernatural explanations, religious beliefs are by their very nature protected to an extraordinary extent from disproof. Magical promises of immediate or concrete rewards are far easier to test, and to disconfirm. Thus, it is neither surprising nor shameful that the majority of human beings find religious beliefs at least plausible and probably somewhat convincing. Our theoretical model, however, observes that humans are never completely certain, and the AI memory discussed in this chapter shackles faith securely to doubt.

This chapter has really been about individual cognition, not social cognition, because the software agents were not exchanging ideas with each other, but only rewards. Our final tasks are to explore the emergence of religious culture, thereby to loop this analysis back to the beginning, and to distill from the entire work a fruitful set of hypotheses.

8

Culture

The final chapter of the book draws together key concepts from the previous chapters, and builds upon the earlier simulations in a way that suggests directions future research may take. We begin by modeling two of the existing theories concerning how novel religions emerge. We will continue to be interested in how faith in supernatural beings arises, but now we will allow the agents to communicate ideas, as if they were exchange partners engaged in theological discussions with each other. Having modeled death, it is time to model birth, and see what happens when a community persists over several generations. The work will be firmly grounded in the existing theory of religion, but we will also begin to articulate new theoretical ideas, suggested by the discipline of computer simulation.

SUBCULTURE EVOLUTION

Theory places great stress upon the social processes that generate and sustain religion, and it doubts the capacity of most individual human beings to create religion in isolation from other believers. The simulation described in the previous chapter modeled relatively credulous agents, because their memory registers started out with numbers more than 10 times the lowest number the computer would allow (an initial random number between 500 and 1,000, compared with a floor of 50). Thus, the emergence of faith in supernatural beings was really the disconfirmation of hope that natural beings could provide the desired reward of life. If people are not credulous to begin with, then they will not develop faith in the gods unless some process can add numbers to the memory registers dedicated to supernatural exchange partners.

The standard theory of religion offers such mechanisms, all involving communication. The theory places great stress on the *explanations* that people offer each other about how to obtain rewards and avoid costs. The simulation can be set so that whenever people complete a successful exchange, they "discuss" some reward that one or both of them have found difficult to obtain. The person with a clearer opinion will influence the one with less confidence. This is easy to do with neural nets. For example, the computer could calculate averages of the two persons' memory registers and place them in the appropriate registers of the person with lower variance across theories. Or the computer could simply have the person with less faith (lower variance across theories) adopt the beliefs of the more confident party to the conversation. Such communication really will help the members of the community achieve successful theories for obtaining available rewards much more quickly than they would do without communication.

This is a key mechanism underpinning the subculture-evolution model of cult formation (Bainbridge and Stark 1979, 291). The principles of the model, as originally stated 25 years ago, are listed here. In chapters 2 and 4 we saw how social processes of encapsulation may occur, important to the later steps of the model, and now we will focus on the exchange of compensators that is central to it. Although the model speaks about cult formation, it uses the term *cult* to refer to a religious movement with novel beliefs or practices, so every novel religion begins as a cult, Buddhism and Christianity included. It applies as well to tribal religions, of which Judaism may be the most sophisticated familiar example, in which case it merely models a longer period of gestation than the cults in modern society that typically emerge in a period of five or ten years.

The Subculture-Evolution Model of Cult Formation

1. Cults are the expression of novel social systems, usually small in size but composed of at least a few intimately interacting individuals.

2. These cultic social systems are most likely to emerge in populations already deeply involved in the occult milieu, but cult evolution may also begin in entirely secular settings.

3. Cults are the result of sidetracked or failed collective attempts to obtain scarce or nonexistent rewards.

4. The evolution begins when a group of persons commits itself to the attainment of certain rewards.

5. In working together to obtain these rewards, members begin exchanging other rewards as well, such as affect.

6. As they progressively come to experience failure in achieving their original goals, they will gradually generate and exchange compensators as well.

7. If the intragroup exchange of rewards and compensators become sufficiently intense, the group will become relatively encapsulated, in the extreme case undergoing complete social implosion.

8. Once separated to some degree from external control, the evolving cult develops and consolidates a novel culture, energized by the need to facilitate the exchange of rewards and compensators, and inspired by essentially accidental factors.

9. The end point of successful cult evolution is a novel religious culture embodied in a distinct social group which must now cope with the problems of extracting resources (including new members) from the environment.

In the subculture-evolution model, an intensely interacting group of individuals commits itself to the attainment of rewards, some of which are very difficult or even impossible to obtain. As they exchange rewards among themselves, they also exchange explanations about how to get other rewards. In the attempt to satisfy each other, they may magnify slightly their positive evaluation of explanations. Those explanations that can be evaluated empirically will be rejected, leaving the nonempirical (supernatural) explanations that cannot readily be evaluated. Faith will spiral upward, and the group will create a folk religion through a series of thousands of tiny communication steps.

There are potentially many aspects and variants of the subculture-evolution model, and here we must limit our explorations to a few simple points. We will run one simulation, similar to that in the previous chapter, to just 100 turns, collecting summary data on the gradual increase in the agents' tendency to place their hopes for eternal life on supernatural exchange partners, rather than natural ones. Then we will run the simulation again, but allow some communication between agents about their faith.

Whenever an economic exchange is successfully achieved, the two agents are presumably pleased with each other. Each views the other as a good source of rewards, and explanations are a sort of reward. They begin to discuss religion, and the one with clearer, more definite beliefs influences the one with weaker beliefs.

Specifically, in terms of the actual computations in the simulation, the conversation begins when the computer looks in the variance memory registers for the life reward of both agents. Whichever of the two has a higher maximum variance is defined as the more confident of the two. The life memory registers of the more confident agent are then copied exactly into the corresponding memory registers of the less confident agent. This is the cognitive version of conversion, which we considered noncognitively in chapters 3 and 4.

After the exchange with the religious discussion, both agents may of course continue to change the contents of some of their life memory registers, reducing the numbers in some cells as they have unrewarding experiences trying to get life from other agents. Therefore, this process is not a simple one of the most confident agent dominating everybody else. Indeed, the agent who received faith from a confident agent may become even more confident after discounting further the value of fellow agents to provide life, and may return to convert the agent who originally was the source of the faith to an even higher level of confidence.

In terms of the community as a whole, being able to communicate faith should accelerate the progressive increase in hope that gods, rather than people, can provide life. Figure 8.1 graphs the early stages, both with and without communication. The height of each curve represents the percentage of the time an agent would tend to seek life from a god (hypothetical agent with a supernatural ID number) rather than from a person (real agent with a natural ID number).

In the beginning, both simulations started at nearly the same level of faith in supernatural beings as source of life, 25.22 percent for the noncommunication simulation, and 25.26 percent for the simulation with communication. At the end of 50 turns, both had risen, but communication achieved 81.20 percent compared with only 36.05 percent in the noncommunication simulation. Then, something drastic happened in the communication simulation, and the curve began to drop. After 100 turns, the difference was far less, 42.29 percent for the communication simulation, and 39.48 for noncommunication.

What happened in the communication condition was quite remarkable! One of the agents, by chance, had started the simulation with two very high numbers in two of the 3-group memory registers, 999 in the Group #1 register, and 976 in the Group #3 register. Again, by chance, as this agent's pattern got communicated and tested, some agent (or chain of agents, during the

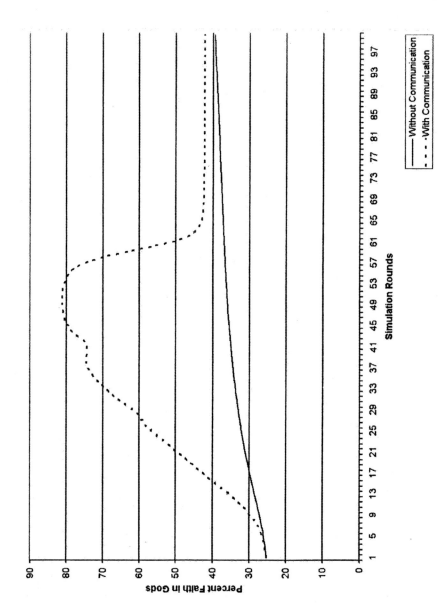

FIGURE 8.1
Subculture Evolution.

communication) failed to test the Group #1 register, but did test Group #0 and Group #2, learning they were wrong and driving their contents down to the minimum permitted in the simulation. This left a pattern with very high variance, asserting there were 3 groups and eternal life could be gotten from both Group #1 and Group #3. The latter of these is supernatural, of course, because the remainder after dividing any number by 3 cannot be 3, in the natural number system. But the remainder after dividing any number by 3 can be 1, and the 999 in the Group #1 register refers to a category of real agents, whose ability to provide eternal life could readily be tested empirically.

Indeed, as agents tried to get additional life from other agents, they would discover this error, and begin reducing the 999 to lower numbers. For example, one such interaction reduced it to 899, but this is still a very high number. Because communication was happening often, as agents exchanged material resources, and the search for eternal life was happening relatively slowly, these intense hopes spread more rapidly than they were debunked. In a way, this is a process of natural selection, in which the most intense faiths spread most rapidly, and depending upon other social conditions may come to dominate the culture, even if they are empirically falsifiable.

Nobody in either simulation was ever actually able to obtain life from a god, or even to see a god. Indeed, an important point is that they were unable to test the hypothesis that a given god could provide eternal life. That nonfalsifiability is the hallmark of supernatural promises. In the communication simulation, the hopes of the most hopeful could spread throughout the community, even faster than their disconfirmation in the period between 50 and 100 turns. Later, as aging agents more often actively sought eternal life and learned that natural agents could not provide it, their hopes shifted toward the supernatural agents we call gods. At the end of 1,000 turns, when we could see the views held by all the agents at the moment of their deaths, 79.33 percent of the hopes of agents in the noncommunication condition were dedicated to gods, and 73.22 percent in the communication condition. Thus, paradoxically, in this experiment communication led to only a temporary increase in faith in gods, over noncommunication.

However, the world of Cyburg is chaotic, just as is the real world. Running the communication experiment again gives markedly different results, merely because of random events. Figure 8.2 graphs the communication simulation again as a dashed line, with 4 other simulations run under exactly the same

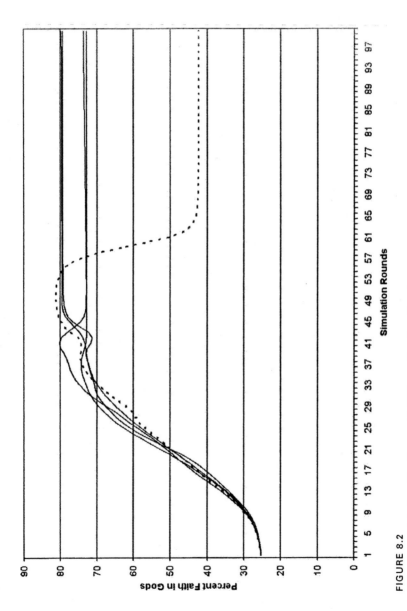

FIGURE 8.2
Subculture Variation: Five Runs with Different Random Numbers.

conditions but with different random numbers. Note that the simulation we described turns out to be atypical. Some kind of crisis point is reached by all five of the simulations at about 40 turns, but the consequences are much milder in the four other simulations. For the five computer runs, the percent faith in gods at 100 turns is 36.05, 72.89, 73.70, 79.31, and 79.38 percent. And after 1,000 turns, it is 73.22, 77.89, 83.95, 84.64, and 85.11. Incidentally, the maximum possible faith in gods is 91.68 percent, given the fact we have set a minimum of 50 points in each memory register, and the numbers in god registers cannot be higher than 999, because this is the top of the range of random numbers we put into them.

One result of communication is the emergence of communities of faith. We will continue to look at the unusual communication simulation, because it represents those interesting cases in which a sect flourishes on the basis of an intense mixture of both general compensators and specific compensators. Specific compensators can be tested empirically, but in their enthusiasm sects may delay doing so.

At the end of just 100 turns, averaging 200 exchanges per agent, the 44,100 different religious viewpoints had collapsed down to just 241 viewpoints that could be identified computationally by tabulating the total variances in the life memory registers. Table 8.1 reports the memberships of the 10 largest. They could be called congregations, because they represent blocs of shared faith sustained by social relationships. However, each has a somewhat distinct set of beliefs, emphasizing one god or another, so it seems reasonable to call

Table 8.1. Subculture Evolution: Ten Largest Denominations

Denomination	After 100 Turns		After 1,000 Turns	
	Number	Percent (%)	Number	Percent (%)
1	34,630	78.53	2,167	4.91
2	1,129	2.56	1,918	4.35
3	1,057	2.40	1,863	4.22
4	937	2.12	1,468	3.33
5	879	1.99	1,420	3.22
6	862	1.95	1,201	2.72
7	855	1.94	889	2.02
8	792	1.80	806	1.83
9	761	1.73	804	1.82
10	111	0.25	792	1.80
TOTAL	42,013	95.27	13,328	30.22

them sects. The largest has fully 34,630 members, or more than 78 percent of Cyburg's residents. Together, the 10 largest denominations account for more than 95 percent of Cyburg's residents.

An additional 14 denominations have 50 or more members each, accounting for another 1,062 members or 2.41 percent. There are 27 groups with 10 or more members, but fewer than 50, accounting for another 647 members or 1.47 percent. Fully 59 groups have between 2 and 9 members, adding 247 members or 0.56 percent. Finally, a total of 131 agents have idiosyncratic viewpoints, for the final approximately 0.3 percent of the population. The distribution of a very few large groups and increasingly more smaller groups fits Zipf's Law (Zipf 1949; Axtell 2001), mentioned in chapter 2, and is comparable to the granularity analysis in chapter 3. If we wanted, we could add principles from those earlier simulations here showing how denominations can consolidate and compete. We already have a key principle from the simulations of chapter 4, because the favorable exchange relationship between two agents, which allows them to discuss theology, constitutes a social bond.

However, once the pattern of activity shifts among the agents, more frequently involving explicit search for eternal life, the dominant sect will begin to lose membership, as individuals disconfirm some of its this-worldly claims for themselves. Table 8.1 also shows the sizes of the top 10 denominations after 1,000 turns. Now, no one sect or denomination dominates Cyburg, and the largest has just under 1/20th of the population. Indeed, the sect that had 34,630 members is no longer the biggest group, and has dropped into 4th place with 1,468 members, having suffered massive defections and the equivalent of schisms as similar but distinct viewpoints have gathered up defectors. The number of viewpoints in the town has increased to 1,827, although 71.19 percent of the population belong to the 76 sects, denominations, or (if you will) congregations with at least 100 members.

PSYCHOPATHOLOGY AND INSPIRATION

A very different model of cult formation, and of the origins of religion, is found in a rather large library of classical essays by anthropologists, psychologists, and psychiatrists, alleging that individual supernatural visions are the result of episodes of individual psychopathology (Freud 1927/1964; Roheim 1955; Wallace 1956; Messing 1958; Lévi-Strauss 1963; Silverman 1967; Lewis 1971; La Barre 1972). The fact that much of this literature was deeply influenced by the psychoanalytic movement, whose status in behavioral science has declined markedly over the past half-century, should not necessarily discredit the idea. For one thing, it draws upon a considerable body of historical and anthropological data for illustrative cases. For another, even as cognitive science establishes itself as the premier discipline to understand individual human behavior, it needs to salvage as much truth as can be found in its predecessors, including depth psychology broadly defined.

The original version of the psychopathology model (Bainbridge and Stark 1979, 285) is listed here. It locates the birth of religion not in the group but in an exceptional individual. A person experiences an episode of mental illness, gaining a random set of wild beliefs. The process of returning to sanity will cause the person to abandon many of these beliefs because they conflict with reality, but the supernatural beliefs will not encounter empirical disconfirmation. If the person regains a position in the society and becomes a trusted exchange partner, he or she will communicate these religious beliefs to others. Not only do our computer simulations model the emergence of a messianic religion perfectly well, but if the community is divided into two parts that do not communicate with each other and psychopathology besets individuals in both parts, then the community will develop two competing denominations with somewhat different beliefs about the identities of the gods.

The Psychopathology Model of Cult Formation

1. Cults are novel cultural responses to personal and societal crisis.
2. New cults are invented by individuals suffering from certain forms of mental illness.
3. These individuals typically achieve their novel visions during psychotic episodes.
4. During such an episode, the individual invents a new package of compensators to meet his own needs.
5. The individual's illness commits him to his new vision, either because his hallucinations appear to demonstrate its truth, or because his compelling needs demand immediate satisfaction.
6. After the episode, the individual will be most likely to succeed in forming a cult around his vision if the society contains many other persons suffering from problems similar to those originally faced by the cult founder, to whose solution, therefore, they are likely to respond.

7. Therefore, such cults most often succeed during times of societal crisis, when large numbers of persons suffer from similar unresolved problems.
8. If the cult does succeed in attracting many followers, the individual founder may achieve at least a partial cure of his illness, because his self-generated compensators are legitimated by other persons, and because he now receives true rewards from his followers.

I have tried modeling the psychiatric episode in several ways, one of which simply uses random numbers to give any individual a small possibility at any time of experiencing an acute psychosis in which a fresh set of big random numbers are poked into the victim's memory registers. For purposes of careful experimentation, it seemed better to add an input module to the software, so the user could inspect the memory registers of any selected agent, and add numbers of experimentally chosen magnitudes to particular memory registers. Thus, we can give an individual the faith that a particular kind of natural agent can provide eternal life, watch the enthusiasm of this agent spread through communications to others, and then see it decline as the agents discover that in fact this explanation does not work.

A simulation modeling psychopathology was done by taking one of the energy-producing agents and adding 2,000 units to the life memory register for the god who belongs to Group #3 when there are two groups. Communication was switched on, so this radical faith could spread from this individual to others. By the end of 100 turns, overall faith in the gods had rocketed from 25.32 percent to 91.24 percent, a very high level of faith. One might predict that such a strong religious movement should also lead to a much quicker consolidation of Cyburg's residents into one dominant denomination, but table 8.2 shows that this is not the case.

Table 8.2 can be compared directly with table 8.1. Here, the largest denomination is just a quarter the size of the largest one produced by the subculture-evolution model. How could this be the case? First, I will explain it in terms of the computer program, then of the human religious phenomena it is meant to represent.

The agent that was given the extremely large number in a god register therefore promulgated with great confidence the theory that there are only two groups of agents, with respect to eternal life. This theory spread rapidly, but because the two-group variance was so high, the converted agents were very

Table 8.2. Messianic Psychopathology: Ten Largest Denominations

Denomination	After 100 Turns		After 1,000 Turns	
	Number	Percent (%)	Number	Percent (%)
1	8,660	19.64	1,290	2.93
2	3,856	8.74	633	1.44
3	1,968	4.46	615	1.39
4	1,276	2.89	565	1.28
5	1,018	2.31	479	1.09
6	1,017	2.31	328	0.74
7	686	1.56	278	0.63
8	665	1.51	249	0.56
9	588	1.33	201	0.46
10	460	1.04	187	0.42
TOTAL	20,194	45.79	4,825	10.94

slow to try other theories (three groups, four groups). When some of them did, they often tried to get life from a natural agent and, in failing, gained a different number in one of their memory registers. This was equivalent to having a slightly different belief system. Coming relatively late in the hundred turns, none of the several variations on the belief system had enough time to become dominant in Cyburg.

In the real world, the early days of religious cults are highly unstable. Some of the most successful of them go through several periods with somewhat different belief systems (see, e.g., Bainbridge 1978). Schisms are common, and rival leaders often depart to form new groups. Researchers of new religious movements are well aware that cults tend to form in families, sharing a number of the same characteristics (Bainbridge 1985a). In reality, as well as in these computer simulations, an evolutionary process takes place (cf. Bainbridge 1997a), as groups diversify, and some among them are able to recruit new members better than others.

At the end of this simulation, after 1,000 turns and after all the agents had died, a census of their beliefs at death indicated there were fully 10,987 viewpoints. The largest denomination had declined from 8,660 members to just 278, and fell to seventh place. I cannot promise that the social processes are identical, but I find it very interesting that these simulations show a significant tendency for defection, fragmentation, or schism after extreme religious views become popular. That is also what I believe I have observed in my field research on radical religious movements, most obvious within the Process, where a substantial number of the individuals I met were devout one-person religious denominations with autarchic systems of beliefs, to the Family where a remarkable diversity of opinion existed on many matters (Bainbridge 1978, 2002). The stereotype that members of radical religious cults have doctrinal uniformity is false. If sects and cults seem to stress uniformity of opinion, perhaps it is precisely because they do not have it, and achieving anything remotely like a consensus in a radical religious group is extremely difficult.

In principle, I can see four ways a wholly new religion can come into being. First, a new religion can grow like a rumor, as individuals in a closely interacting group communicate with each other, progressively amplifying their hopes until they become a faith. This is the *subculture-evolution model*. In actual human society, rumors follow rumors in quick succession, and it is frankly hard to see how the process can stabilize to produce a very precise and long-lasting set of beliefs and practices. Presumably, no one model need stand alone, however, and other processes may institutionalize a religion once it has come into being.

Second, a person may suffer an episode of emotionally powerful delusions and subsequently convince other people to share them. This is the *psychopathology model* of cult formation. Clearly, the founder must endure a very tricky series of situations, experiencing visions only for a limited period of time and becoming socially competent afterward. For any given individual, success is unlikely. But by the law of large numbers, a few cases will succeed, and they will contribute immeasurably to the world's sacred culture.

Third, someone may perceive an opportunity to gain riches or other rewards by offering a new faith to people who need one. I have called this the *entrepreneur model* of cult formation (Bainbridge and Stark 1979), and it likens the creation of a religion either to the establishment of a business or to the practice of engineering. Every other kind of culture in modern societies is consciously engineered, but we are not used to thinking about religion in this way. I have not included this model within Cyburg, but M. Afzal Upal at the University of Toledo (Ohio) has been experimenting with computer simulations of a very different design to explore implications of the entrepreneur model.

Fourth, a real god that actually exists may choose to communicate a new perception of his or her nature to humans, selecting a particular leader or set of leaders to guide mankind into this new dispensation. This final alternative recognizes the logical possibility that a new religion may simply be true. While it leaves room for some sociological theory, at the stage when the religion grows via recruitment of new members, it is not strictly a social or cognitive theory of the origins of a religion, and therefore it does not give us a fourth model to simulate.

FAMILY INHERITANCE

One of the striking facts about the major religions of the world is that their full development took centuries, even in those cases in which substantial recruitment of members occurred during the lifetime of the founders. Thus, simulations that end with a single lifetime are too limited. Fortunately, it is easy to model reproduction in the present software. I have set Cyburg to have room for only 44,100 people, and we fill it up at the beginning of the simulations described here and in the previous chapter. However, around the 500th turn, members begin to die. In the simulation just described in the previous section, already 227 had died after 500 turns. The march to the grave continued: after 600 turns, 8,852 had died; 700 turns, 17,648; 800 turns, 26,421; 900 turns, 35,308. After 1,000 turns, all 44,100 agents had expired. Among other things, this meant that there was room for new agents after the 500th turn.

With the reproduction option switched on, the simulation adds a sixth reward to the existing 5 (energy, water, food, oxygen, life), namely, sex. Agents learn that when their sexual satisfaction is low, they can gain satisfaction by interacting with a member of the opposite sex. The sexes are marked by the division into odd ID numbers and even ID numbers, so for sex there really are two groups of agents. If a couple engages in sex, and there is an open home in Cyburg, their child is placed there. Education occurs instantly by giving the child a mixture of the parents' memory registers for the first five rewards. Specifically, the program determines which parent has a greater variance of memory registers for a given reward, and copies that parent's data into the child's memory registers. This would not work well for sex itself, because erotic partners are sex-specific in this simulation, so I had the computer give the child random numbers in the same range as the original agents received at their births.

The first thing to report is that this process works. In fact, the population of Cyburg stays fairly close to the maximum 44,100 population indefinitely. The simulation to be described momentarily was run for 5,000 turns, and during that time fully 273,195 agents lived and died in the town, and the town was full of living agents when the simulation ended.

The point of this simulation was not to test a particular well-defined hypothesis, but mainly to demonstrate that such a complex system could in fact

Table 8.3. Evolution of Religion in a Multigeneration Community

	After 100 Turns	After 1,000 Turns	After 5,000 Turns
Membership of 10 largest denominations	15,989	10,424	39,469
Membership as percentage	36.3%	23.6%	89.5%
Total number of viewpoints	2,889	20,177	587
Mean viewpoint adherents	15.3	2.2	75.1
Number of viewpoints with a single adherent	1,512	14,396	318

be self-sustaining. This simulation does, however, pull out all the stops on communication. The communication option was switched on, as in the two previous simulations, but with geographic limitations. Cyburg was divided into four quadrants with 11,025 agents in each. Agents were allowed to exchange rewards (and have sex) freely with agents in their own quadrant or in any of the other three. But they discussed religion only with exchange partners in this own neighborhood. Religious beliefs could cross from one quadrant to another only when a child was born, because three-quarters of the time the child would live as an adult in a different quadrant from the parent with the stronger religious faith. Our main goal in this simulation was to achieve a high degree of complexity. Table 8.3 shows how the number and memberships of denominations changed over the course of this multigeneration simulation.

Fundamentally, this is a replay of the subculture-evolution model. From 100 turns to 1,000 turns, the larger denominations lose membership and religious consensus fragments. But from 1,000 turns to 5,000, with intergenerational transmission of faith and much time for viewpoints to die out, a major religious consolidation takes place. The largest denomination winds up with 10,154 members, just under a quarter of Cyburg's population. The next three denominations are nearly as large: 9,494, 9,327, and 8,640. The six others that have more than 200 members round out the top ten: 454, 401, 307, 244, 227, and 221. Only 318 agents have idiosyncratic belief systems. Thus we see the importance of developing simulations that run for a long time, especially for many generations, in order to model the multigenerational nature of enduring faiths.

SOCIAL CLASS AND RELIGIOUS COMPENSATORS

It is well known that religious sects, or denominations that cater to relatively deprived persons such as the lower social classes, tend to be more fervent in their

hopes for divine aid (Stark and Bainbridge 1987; Bainbridge 1997a). Specifically, deprived people are more likely to accept supernatural compensators for
rewards that exist but which they personally lack. Quite separately from the
Cyburg simulations, I wrote a small program using a very different memory
system to explore the greater tendency of deprived persons to prefer sectarian
forms of religion.

Let us imagine that this simulation concerns a suburb of Cyburg, with room
for 100 residents. I could have called this village Cyburb, but decided Compton
(computer town) was more dignified for a subdivision. Initially, there are only
50 agents. Similar to earlier simulations, 10 of them produce energy, 10 water,
10 food, and 10 oxygen, but the remaining 10 constitute an underclass that
lacks an important economic function. After a while, romantic attachments
are formed and babies are born. Then, the older agents begin to die, making
room for more babies. So, although Compton has room for only 100 agents
at any given time, this particular simulation involves more than five times that
number who were residents at one time or another.

Instead of using an approach inspired by neural nets, I wrote the program
to include the names of as many as 100 actual people and 4 gods. The rules for
an exchange partner memory register are simple:

1. When an agent decides to seek a particular reward, the agent consults an
   appropriate exchange partner memory register.
2. If a consulted register is empty, the agent guesses a name from the master
   list at random and puts it in the register.
3. When an agent consults a register containing a name, the agent seeks an
   exchange with the agent bearing that name.
4. If an agent named refuses a trade, the name is removed from the register.
5. If an agent has two or more names in memory registers for the desired
   reward, the agent chooses among them at random.

The presence of a name in a register represents the hypothesis that the
person named can supply the desired reward, whether the hypothesis is based
on past experience or pure guesswork. In terms of the theory of religion, such
a hypothesis is a *specific explanation*, a particular statement about how a given
reward can be obtained.

Often, an agent's hypothesis will be a poor one, but to some extent they can learn from experience. Axiom 4 ("Human action is directed by a complex but finite information-processing system that functions to identify problems and attempt solutions to them.") applies to them, as it does to us, although our capacity to learn is much greater than theirs. Clearly, they start out almost completely ignorant about the world they live in, and they have limited ability to learn the laws of its nature. Unlike the agents discussed earlier in this chapter and in chapter 7, they are completely incapable of categorizing exchange partners, and merely learn individual names. One reason for using a completely different learning system is to show that results from earlier simulations were not merely artifacts of the way the program was written. Another reason was to have a system in which it was possible for faith in gods to range all the way from 0 percent up to 100 percent. I believe there are many ways to program neural nets or other machine learning systems to represent faith in supernatural beings, and in this chapter I offer two.

What happens if one of these agents puts the name of one of the four gods in a memory register, hypothesizing that this named entity can provide a reward? One thing which does not happen is for the god to refuse the trade. Within the world of the simulation, the gods do not exist, only their names. So the hypothesis is not disconfirmed by the agent's attempt to exchange with the god, and the name remains in the memory register. If another agent initiates a successful exchange with the first agent, the second agent's name may replace the name of the god in the first agent's memory. But until such a factually rewarding exchange does displace the god's name, the agent will continue to hypothesize that the god would be a good source of a particular reward.

With respect to the community of agents in Compton, the four extra names refer to supernatural beings. They can imagine one of these entities and carry out the initial stages of an exchange with it, but they cannot complete the exchange within the natural world defined by the program. In the language of the theory of religion, the hypothesis that one of these four gods can provide a reward is a *compensator*. Thus, in a modest way, this simulation, like the others described in the two concluding chapters of this book, successfully incorporates the concept of compensators, which is the fulcrum of the theory of religion.

In table 8.4 we can see the result of a simulation that was run for 200,000 exchanges, spanning several generations. A total of 520 persons lived their

Table 8.4. Social Class and Religious Faith

	Upper Class	Middle Class	Lower Class
Number of agents	103	314	103
Average wealth at death	15,713	3,339	1,036
Percent of memory registers containing names at death	95.6%	94.3%	80.7%
Percent of these names which are gods, for:			
Supplies	6.6%	13.5%	38.2%
Romance	38.0%	41.1%	49.3%
Life	100.0%	100.0%	100.0%

lives, died, and upon meeting their maker (me) printed out the complete contents of their memory registers. There were 103 upper-class energy producers; 314 middle-class producers of water, food, and oxygen; and 103 lower-class unemployed persons. The average wealth of energy barons at death was 15,713 units of energy, water, food, and oxygen—5 times the middle-class average and 15 times the lower-class average. A fifth of the poor agents' memory registers were empty, a sign of the difficulties they faced finding willing exchange partners, while 95.6 percent of rich agents' memory registers contained the names of exchange partners.

The lower half of the table shows the extent to which agents hoped gods would provide them with a desired reward, instead of having the names of fellow Compton residents in the memory registers. Members of the lower class were especially likely to seek supplies from supernatural sources, 38.2 percent of the time. In contrast, upper-class residents had a god's name rather than a person's name in a supply memory register only 6.6 percent of the time.

The difference is less great, but in the same direction, for romance. The poor can love each other, even if they cannot make each other rich, but their economic deprivations limit romantic opportunities in the small society of Compton.

For life, which cannot be provided by humans, only gods are appropriate exchange partners. The three social classes are equally deprived with respect to immortality. Thus, an identical 100 percent of memory registers containing the names of potential life-giving partners refer to gods.

Although random factors affected each of the 200,000 exchanges of the simulation, the general pattern of results is strictly determined by the assumptions on which the program was written. But the results are nowhere stated in the program. Rather, the computer has deduced them. When the program is repeated, the outcome is a slightly different set of numbers but the same general pattern. The results can be described by two propositions from the theory; or conversely it may be said that the simulation has derived these propositions (Stark and Bainbridge 1987, 43–44):

P25 The power of an individual or group is negatively associated with accepting religious compensators, when the desired reward exists.

P26 Regardless of power, persons and groups tend to accept religious compensators, when desired rewards do not exist.

FORMULATING HYPOTHESES

The creator of theory-based computer simulations often learns as much from writing them as from running them, because the programming requires one to think deeply about one's own ideas. It would not be much of an exaggeration to say that simulating gives one an entirely different perspective on the world as a chaotic, constantly adjusting system, in which multiple factors play constantly with changing conditions. In such a context, it can often be difficult to distinguish inputs from outputs, and assumptions from findings. But if the point is to facilitate thought, this may not matter.

Below are 19 of the hypotheses postulated here in the light of results from computer simulations. Many of these are not new ideas, although they take on new significance in the context of computer simulation. They are not listed in any strict order, because the ones introduced in early chapters often gained clarity from later chapters. Nor am I claiming to have proven these hypotheses, either logically or empirically. Rather, they suggest questions for future empirical research, and reflect the kind of thinking facilitated by computer simulation of religion.

H1 The results of social interaction are often very different from what the interacting individuals would have intended or expected.

H2 A religious movement that practices outreach, intentionally developing social bonds with nonmembers, may either gain or lose depending upon the balance of social influences toward or away from the group.

H3 An actively recruiting religious movement can grow rapidly through concentration of forces, even if it is initially quite small, by maneuvering itself into being a local majority.

H4 The fates of particular religious organizations and movements are to a significant degree the results of pure chance.

H5 Many social and cultural religious structures can be explained as the result of processes of chaotic aggregation in self-organizing systems, rather than conscious design, human nature, or some higher-level principle of organization.

H6 A religious movement that becomes encapsulated, lacking many social bonds with nonmembers, is likely to suffer stagnation and decline.

H7 Cooperation may exist without religion, but religion can facilitate cooperation by providing incentives and by establishing the reputations of potential exchange partners.

H8 The human mind can solve many difficult problems, but its solutions are always suboptimal.

H9 Religious beliefs are the result of the same processes of learning, problem solving, and communication that guide human behavior outside the realm of the sacred.

H10 Beliefs are always held more or less tentatively, because any mind capable of solving many different problems will be aware of alternative possible solutions to all of them.

H11 People in different social locations experience very different worlds, some more complex and unstable than others, and thus they require greater or lesser cognitive effort to master their situations.

H12 Learning effectively improves our ability to extract rewards from the environment, but learning is both inconsistent and incomplete.

H13 Religious faith can emerge through a series of communications, in which individuals imperceptibly exaggerate their confidence in the ideas they exchange.

H14 Religious faith can begin when a single individual experiences random, meaningless, or psychopathological learning, then transmits a new doctrine to other individuals.

H15 Extreme beliefs can become highly popular if they spread socially via communication more rapidly than they are debunked within the experience of individuals.

H16 Rapid diffusion of extreme, supernatural beliefs tends to lead to defection, schism, and fragmentation rather than unification of religious culture.

H17 Any strongly held religious faith is a local minimum, superior in some way to very similar faiths, but ultimately suboptimal if not false.

H18 Consolidation, transformation, or erosion of religious culture is typically a very slow process, requiring many generations.

H19 The ability of computers to simulate religious faith and many related phenomena suggests that religion does not depend upon the actual existence of the supernatural.

Religion, in the context of these insights, is both natural and unnatural. It is natural that humans want the sense of security that conviction can provide, yet any particular set of religious beliefs is largely arbitrary. The paradox of religion is immediately apparent in the fact that there are so many different religions, and there have been many more so across the full sweep of human history. Consensus supports conviction, but consensus about the supernatural—in the absence of direct and undeniable input from the supernatural itself—is always breaking down.

THE COGNITIVE SCIENCE OF RELIGION

As cognitive science has been created over the past 30 years, one of the major disciplines that studies religious belief has been absent without leave, namely, sociology. This is literally a tragic situation, because sociology had much to offer, and by sulking like Achilles in its tent, it has been rendered impotent. Perhaps there are several explanations why most fields of sociology have progressed little over that period of time, but one clearly is sociology's general refusal to collaborate with other disciplines.

Evolutionary theories of cognition, such as those influential in the cognitive anthropology of religion, assume that general explanations (mental tools, schemas) have been wired into the human brain. The Stark-Bainbridge theory (learning, rational choice) argues, in contrast, that general explanations are socially constructed generalizations from specific explanations. In fact, both views may be correct, in that the mental structures that have been wired into the brain by evolution require learning to become effective, and further learning can combine them and add to them. Only research can determine which mental tools are innate, which are learned, and how the processes of inheritance and learning interact to form human thought and determine behavior. That research is likely to require the efforts of many scientists, across numerous fields, working collaboratively for decades.

The debate will be similar to one within the field of artificial intelligence. On the one side are neural network researchers, like myself, whose work emphasizes bottom-up machine learning from which higher-level principles spontaneously emerge. On the other side are researchers who design cognitive architectures composed of higher-level principles that can be assembled into production systems, for example, in the form of chains of if-then propositions, which then are applied downward to specific situations. The question is not which is more effective or which provides a better description of the human brain. Presumably, both are needed. So the real question for future work is how to combine them.

Importantly, we do not really know how many fundamental schemas are central to human mental nature, what happens when they contradict each other, and how they shape religious cognition. Most of the anthropologists and psychologists working in the field assert, on the basis of fairly good evidence, that one of the fundamental schemas predisposes people to attribute mind and intention to complex phenomena (Atran 2002; Boyer 2002; Barrett 2004). That is, humans tend to conceptualize complex phenomena as agents having mentality similar to their own. This tendency probably contributes greatly to religious beliefs. However, humans are also capable of conceptualizing complex phenomena mechanically, without resorting to supernatural assumptions.

Learning probably plays a role in determining when an individual will attribute agency to events, rather than seeing them as having mechanical or random origins. Much of this learning is social, and it is a notable fact that the religious traditions of the world emerged over extended periods of time through social interaction. However, much human learning occurs through personal interaction with material systems, including technology. The invention of the mechanical clock, and more recently of the electronic computer, provided everyone with examples of complex systems that lacked souls.

Quite apart from the possibility that changing technologies and other world conditions may weaken the mental module that inspires people to attribute souls or agency to complex systems, the existence of such a module cannot itself explain religion, as it manifested itself in historical times or as it exists today. The agency module in the human mind may have evolved to help humans identify prey or predators in prehistoric environments, or it may have emerged in connection with the development of social life among members of hunter-gatherer bands over a million years of evolution. In either case, it is only very indirectly related to monotheism or to modern religious bureaucracies.

Logically, such a module or mental schema would support the assumption that there are many minor supernatural beings, just as there were many different predators and humans in the prehistoric world. I would suggest that two other modules are important, but that the three are only the beginning for identifying the facts that gave rise to modern religions. One other module is the general explanation that humans who are unable to attain rewards by themselves should seek cooperation with other humans to obtain them. The other schema is the magical assumption that human wishes and intentions can somehow directly influence the material world.

Nearly 20 years ago, Stark and I (Stark and Bainbridge 1987, 112–13) offered a purely cognitive theory of the emergence of monotheism (or, more precisely, dualism), that suggested the number of postulated supernatural beings declined over historical time because fewer gods offer a more parsimonious explanation of the human condition. However, I have never been very confident in that analysis. Conversely, one could argue that polytheism offers a more realistic explanation, one more readily confirmed by experience, because the world, in fact, is affected by many contradictory forces.

Perhaps the triumph of one god over others is simply the doctrinal reflection of the triumph of a particular religious bureaucracy over others. Interestingly, the Bible does not deny that other supernatural forces exist, insisting instead that Jehovah is the one such power deserving worship by the Hebrews. Much of the history of religion may simply be the result of the attempts on the part of religious specialists (priests, messiahs, and the like) to gain power over other people. Consolidation of divinity into one god facilitates consolidation of the priesthood into one organization. Suppression of magic marginalizes independent magicians and healers. Denial of direct contact between the laity and divinity increases the mediatory role of the priesthood. Modern doctrines may be a political compromise between beliefs that give great power to priests, and those that mitigate that power in order to prevent rebellion from people who might feel oppressed by the priests.

All this is to suggest that the anthropologists and psychologists who have pioneered the development of the cognitive science of religion now need to be joined by sociologists. This book immodestly announces that sociology is now present in cognitive science, accounted for, and ready for duty. This book also introduces artificial intelligence, which is already part of cognitive science, to the study of religion.

SUMMATION

The potential of computer simulations in the social science of religion is great. Here, we have intentionally examined a wide range of questions, but still the scope of this book is far less than the religious simulation discipline we could create in the coming years. An optimistic scenario for creating such a discipline is as follows. First, a number of independently working individuals would attempt to simulate religious phenomena, using different computing methods and drawing upon different social-scientific or cognitive theories. Their programs are likely to be very different in structure, user interface, output, and even programming language or environment. As they discuss their results in scientific meetings and in print, they would begin to share programming modules. At some point, they would launch a conscious effort to develop shared, open-source software not only for use by themselves and by students but also to provide a solid basis for interacting with those who use computer simulation in different fields.

Frankly, the social science of religion is somewhat at a disadvantage in the realm of simulation, because its traditions tend to be qualitative—whether historical, observational, or theological—and even quantitative researchers in the field employ off-the-shelf commercial analysis software, rather than writing their own. Thus, only in rare cases will a single individual have the skills to work effectively in this field, until such future time as we actually train people to do it. Therefore, interdisciplinary collaborations will be necessary, bringing together perhaps a religious studies scholar, a cognitive scientist or sociologist, and a computer scientist.

There is much to be said for selecting narrow, well-defined research topics, and writing simulation programs that are lean and free of distracting frills. If too many things are happening at once in a simulation, it is difficult to know how to attribute the outcome. In addition, the more complex a program it is, the more difficult to debug it. I am quite certain that bugs remain in my own software—I just don't know what or where they are. It seemed to me more important to produce a rich and reasonably rigorous demonstration of how computer simulation could inform the study of religion than to achieve perfection in writing every single line of programming code.

Indeed, the other side of the program complexity issue is that most really interesting religious phenomena require a good deal of complexity before they manifest themselves. Having suggested two ways in which machine learning could handle the distinction between natural and supernatural beings, I would very much like to see other options suggested by other researchers.

Another important issue for simulation of religion is how we can best bring theory-based modeling and empirical data analysis together. In some of the physical sciences, it is quite usual to compare the results of a simulation directly with a set of data from the real world. For the scientific study of religion, this is not merely a challenge of writing realistic simulations but also of finding a way to collect data that are sufficiently detailed, ample, and relevant to people's real social-psychological experiences, to make strict comparison possible. One reason I kept returning to censuses of denominations and the shape of their membership size distribution is that comparable real data are available, and future studies can reasonably attempt to model those data closely.

Artificial intelligence is not limited to theory-based simulations but can also be used to model empirical data. Actually, AI methods currently permeate information technology, but usually without the AI label being attached. Especially promising are the techniques of machine learning and data clustering employed by today's search engines and by software for automatic classification of written text. So much religious cognition has been recorded in written documents that a truly immense scientific opportunity awaits those who are willing to learn the necessary methodologies.

Computer simulation is a way of thinking, and thus a tool for theory building and refinement. But computer simulation of religion is also in harmony with the spirit of the early 21st century, as we approach what Ray Kurzweil (1999) called *The Age of Spiritual Machines.* Information technology and cognitive science are rapidly converging with nanotechnology and biotechnology to form a unified scientific-technical culture (Roco and Bainbridge 2002; Roco and Montemagno 2004; Bainbridge and Roco 2006). If religion is going to be a vigorous part of that new, dominant culture, it will need strong connections to computation, information systems, and the science of cognition.

References

Adorno, T. W., Else Frenkel-Brunswik, Daniel J. Levinson, and R. Nevitt Sanford. 1950. *The Authoritarian Personality*. New York: Harper.

Allen, William Sheridan. 1965. *The Nazi Seizure of Power: The Experience of a Single German Town 1930–1933*. Chicago: Quadrangle.

Allport, Gordon. 1954. *The Nature of Prejudice*. Boston: Beacon.

Atran, Scott. 2002. *In Gods We Trust: The Evolutionary Landscape of Religion*. Oxford: Oxford University Press.

Arthur, George Compton Archibald. 1920. *Life of Lord Kitchener*. London: Macmillan.

Axelrod, Robert. 1984. *The Evolution of Cooperation*. New York: Basic Books.

Axtell, Robert L. 2001. Zipf Distribution of U.S. Firm Sizes. *Science* 293:1818–20.

Bainbridge, William Folwell. 1882a. *Along the Lines at the Front*. Philadelphia: American Baptist Publication Society.

———. 1882b. *Around the World Tour of Christian Missions: A Universal Survey*. New York: C. R. Blackall.

———. 1883. *Self-Giving: A Story of Christian Missions*. Boston: D. Lothrup.

Bainbridge, William Sims. 1978. *Satan's Power: Ethnography of a Deviant Psychotherapy Cult*. Berkeley: University of California Press.

———. 1984. Computer Simulations of Cultural Drift. *Journal of the British Interplanetary Society* 37:420–29.

———. 1985a. Cultural Genetics. In *Religious Movements*, edited by Rodney Stark, 157–98. New York: Paragon.

———. 1985b. *Experiments in Sociology*. Belmont, Calif.: Wadsworth.

———. 1986. *Experiments in Psychology*. Belmont, Calif.: Wadsworth.

———. 1987. *Sociology Laboratory*. Belmont, Calif.: Wadsworth.

———. 1989a. Religious Ecology of Deviance. *American Sociological Review* 54:288–95.

———. 1989b. *Survey Research: A Computer-Assisted Introduction.* Belmont, Calif.: Wadsworth.

———. 1990. Explaining the Church Member Rate. *Social Forces* 68:1287–96.

———. 1992a. *Social Research Methods and Statistics.* Belmont, Calif.: Wadsworth.

———. 1992b. The Sociology of Conversion. In *Handbook of Religious Conversion,* edited by H. Newton Malony and Samuel Southard, 178–91. Birmingham, Ala.: Religious Education Press.

———. 1994. Values. In *The Encyclopedia of Language and Linguistics,* edited by R. E. Asher, 4888–92. Oxford: Pergamon.

———. 1995a. Minimum Intelligent Neural Device: A Tool for Social Simulation. *Mathematical Sociology* 20:179–92.

———. 1995b. Neural Network Models of Religious Belief. *Sociological Perspectives* 38:483–95.

———. 1997a. *The Sociology of Religious Movements.* New York: Routledge.

———. 1997b. The Omicron Point: Sociological Application of the Anthropic Theory. In *Chaos and Complexity in Sociology: Myths, Models and Theory,* edited by Raymond A. Eve, Sara Horsfall, and Mary E. Lee, 91–101. Thousand Oaks, Calif.: Sage.

———. 2002. A Prophet's Reward: Dynamics of Religious Exchange. In *Sacred Markets, Sacred Canopies,* edited by Ted G. Jelen, 63–89. Lanham, Md.: Rowman and Littlefield.

———. 2003. Sacred Algorithms: Exchange Theory of Religious Claims. In *Defining Religion,* edited by David Bromley and Larry Greil, 21–37. Amsterdam: JAI Elsevier.

Bainbridge, William Sims, Edward E. Brent, Kathleen M. Carley, David R. Heise, Michael W. Macy, Barry Markovsky, and John Skvoretz. 1994. Artificial Social Intelligence. *Annual Review of Sociology* 20:407–36.

Bainbridge, William Sims, and Mihail C. Roco. 2006. *Managing Nano-Bio-Info-Cogno Innovations: Converging Technologies in Society.* Berlin: Springer.

Bainbridge, William Sims, and Rodney Stark. 1979. Cult Formation: Three Compatible Models. *Sociological Analysis* 40:283–95.

———. 1984. Formal Explanation of Religion: A Progress Report. *Sociological Analysis* 45:145–58.

Barrett, Justin L. 2004. *Why Would Anyone Believe in God?* Walnut Creek, Calif.: AltaMira.

Blau, Judith R., Kenneth C. Land, and Kent Redding. 1992. The Expansion of Religious Affiliation: An Explanation of the Growth of Church Participation in the United States, 1850–1930. *Social Science Research* 21:329–52.

Blau, Judith R., Kent Redding, and Kenneth C. Land. 1993. Ethnocultural Cleavages and the Growth of Church Membership in the United States, 1860–1930. *Sociological Forum* 8:609–37.

Blau, Peter M. 1964. *Exchange and Power in Social Life.* New York: Wiley.

Bloom, Paul. 2004. *Descartes' Baby: How the Science of Child Development Explains What Makes Us Human.* New York: Basic Books.

Bloor, David. 1991. Can There Be an Alternative Mathematics? In *Knowledge and Social Imagery,* edited by D. Bloor, 107–30. Chicago, Ill.: University of Chicago Press.

Boudon, Raymond. 1981. *The Logic of Social Action.* London: Routledge & Kegan Paul.

Boyer, Pascal. 2002. *Religion Explained: The Evolutionary Origins of Religious Thought.* New York: Basic Books.

Bradbury, Ray. 1950. *The Martian Chronicles.* Garden City, N.Y.: Doubleday.

Breault, Kevin D. 1989a. New Evidence on Religious Pluralism, Urbanism, and Religious Participation. *American Sociological Review* 54:1048–53.

———. 1989b. A Reexamination of the Relationship between Religious Diversity and Religious Adherents. *American Sociological Review* 54:1056–59.

Brown, Frederic. 1954. *Angels and Spaceships.* New York: E. P. Dutton.

Burgess, Robert L., and Ronald Akers. 1966. A Differential Association—Reinforcement Theory of Criminal Behavior. *Social Problems* 14:128–47.

Carley, Kathleen M., and David M. Svoboda. 1996. Modeling Organizational Adaptation as a Simulated Annealing Process. *Sociological Methods and Research* 25:138–68.

Carr, Michael H. 1981. *The Surface of Mars.* New Haven, Conn.: Yale University Press.

Christiano, K. J. 1987. *Religious Diversity and Social Change.* Cambridge: Cambridge University Press.

Churchill, Winston S. 1902. *The River War.* London: Longmans, Green.

Cloward, Richard A., and Lloyd Ohlin. 1960. *Delinquency and Opportunity.* New York: Free Press.

Cohen, Albert K. 1955. *Delinquent Boys.* New York: Free Press.

Collins, Randall. 1993. A Theory of Religion. *Journal for the Scientific Study of Religion* 32:402–6.

Cooper, Henry S. F. 1981. *The Search for Life on Mars.* New York: Holt, Rinehart, & Winston.

Crevier, Daniel. 1993. *AI: The Tumultuous History of the Search for Artificial Intelligence.* New York: Basic Books.

d'Aquili, Eugene, and Andrew Newberg. 2000. The Neuropsychology of Aesthetic, Spiritual, and Mystical States. *Zygon* 35:39–52.

de Morgan, Augustus. 1956 Assorted Paradoxes. In *The World of Mathematics,* edited by James R. Newman, 2369–82. New York: Simon & Schuster.

Dollard, John, Neil E. Miller, Leonard W. Doob, O. H. Mowrer, and Robert R. Sears. 1939. *Frustration and Aggression.* New Haven, Conn.: Yale University Press.

Durkheim, Emile. 1897/1951. *Suicide.* New York: Free Press.

Epstein, Joshua M., and Robert Axtell. 1996. *Growing Artificial Societies: Social Science from the Bottom Up*. Washington, D.C.: Brookings Institution Press.

Eve, Raymond A., Sara Horsfall, and Mary E. Lee, eds. 1997. *Chaos and Complexity in Sociology: Myths, Models and Theory*. Thousand Oaks, Calif.: Sage.

Faris, Robert E. L., and H. Warren Dunham. 1939. *Mental Disorders in Urban Areas*. Chicago, Ill.: University of Chicago Press.

Festinger, Leon. 1957. *Theory of Cognitive Dissonance*. Evanston, Ill.: Row, Peterson.

Festinger, Leon, Henry W. Riecken, and Stanley Schachter. 1956. *When Prophecy Fails*. Minneapolis: University of Minnesota Press.

Finke, Roger. 1989. Demographics of Religious Participation: An Ecological Approach, 1850–1980. *Journal for the Scientific Study of Religion* 28:45–58.

Finke, Roger, and Rodney Stark. 1986. Turning Pews into People: Estimating 19th Century Church Membership. *Journal for the Scientific Study of Religion* 25:180–92.

———. 1988. Religious Economies and Sacred Canopies: Religious Mobilization in American Cities, 1906. *American Sociological Review* 53:41–49.

———. 1989a. How the Upstart Sects Won America: 1776–1850. *Journal for the Scientific Study of Religion* 28:27–44.

———. 1989b. Evaluating the Evidence: Religious Economies and Sacred Canopies. *American Sociological Review* 54: 1054–56.

———. 1992. *The Churching of America: 1776–1990*. New Brunswick, N.J.: Rutgers University Press.

Freud, Sigmund. 1927/1964. *The Future of an Illusion*. Garden City, N.Y.: Doubleday.

Garson, G. D. 1991. A Comparison of Neural Network and Expert Systems Algorithms with Common Multivariate Procedures for Analysis of Social Science Data. *Social Science Computer Review* 9:399–434.

Gergen, Kenneth J. 1969. *The Psychology of Behavior Exchange*. Reading, Mass.: Addison-Wesley.

Gibbon, Edward. 1896. *The History of the Decline and Fall of the Roman Empire*. 7 vols. London: Methuin. (Original work published in 1776–1778).

Gilbert, Nigel, and Rosaria Conte, eds. 1995. *Artificial Societies: The Computer Simulation of Social Life*. London: University College London Press.

Gilbert, Nigel, and Jim Doran, eds. 1994. *Simulating Societies: The Computer Simulation of Social Phenomena*. London: University College London Press.

Gleick, James. 1987. *Chaos*. New York: Penguin.

Glock, Charles Y., and Rodney Stark. 1965. *Religion and Society in Tension*. Chicago, Ill.: Rand McNally.

Goerner, Sally J. 1994. *Chaos and the Evolving Ecological Universe*. Luxembourg: Gordon and Breach.

Granovetter, Mark. 1973. The Strength of Weak Ties. *American Journal of Sociology* 78:1360–80.

Hanneman, Robert. 1988. *Computer-Assisted Theory Building.* Newbury Park, Calif.: Sage.

———. 1995. Simulation Modeling and Theoretical Analysis in Sociology. *Sociological Perspectives* 38:457–62.

Hao, Bai-Lin, ed. 1984. *Chaos.* Singapore: World Scientific.

Heider, Fritz. 1958. *The Psychology of Interpersonal Relations.* New York: Wiley.

Herrnstein, Richard J. 1971. Quantitative Hedonism. *Journal of Psychiatric Research* 8:399–412.

Hinton, G. E. 1992. How Neural Networks Learn from Experience. *Scientific American* 267, no. 3: 145–51.

Hinton, G. E., D. C. Plaut, and T. Shallice. 1993. Simulating Brain Damage. *Scientific American* 269, no. 4: 76–82.

Hirschi, Travis. 1969. *Causes of Delinquency.* Berkeley: University of California Press.

Homans, George Caspar. 1950. *The Human Group.* New York: Harcourt, Brace & World.

———. 1967. *The Nature of Social Science.* New York: Harcourt, Brace & World.

———. 1974. *Social Behavior: Its Elementary Forms.* New York: Harcourt, Brace Jovanovich.

Hopgood, Adrian A. 2001. *Intelligent Systems for Engineers and Scientists.* Boca Raton, Fla.: CRC.

Hostetler, John A. 1993. *Amish Life.* Baltimore, Md.: Johns Hopkins University Press.

Hostetler, John A., and Gertrude Enders Huntington. 1996. *The Hutterites in North America.* Fort Worth, Tex.: Harcourt Brace.

Huntington, Samuel P. 1996. *The Clash of Civilizations and the Remaking of World Order.* New York: Simon & Schuster.

Huntley, D. G. 1991. Neural Nets: An Approach to the Forecasting of Time Series. *Social Science Computer Review* 9:27–38.

Jelen, Ted. G., ed. 2002. *Sacred Markets, Sacred Canopies.* Lanham, Md.: Rowman and Littlefield.

Johnson, Eugene C., and H. Gilman McCann. 1982. Acyclic Triplets and Social Structure in Complete Signed Digraphs. *Social Networks* 3:251–72.

Johnson, Spencer. 2002. *Who Moved My Cheese?* New York: G. P. Putnam's Sons.

Johnson, Todd M., and David B. Barrett. 2004. Quantifying Alternate Futures of Religion and Religions. *Futures* 36, no. 9: 947–60.

Kaminka, Gal A. 2004. Multi-agent Systems. In *Berkshire Encyclopedia of Human-Computer Interaction,* edited by William Sims Bainbridge, 475–80. Great Barrington, Mass.: Berkshire.

Karayiannis, N. B., and A. N. Venetsanopoulos. 1993. *Artificial Neural Networks: Learning Algorithms, Performance Evaluation, and Applications.* Boston: Kluwer.

Kassarjian, Harold H., and Thomas S. Robertson. 1981. *Perspectives in Consumer Behavior.* Glenview, Ill.: Scott, Foresman.

Katz, Elihu, and Paul Lazarsfeld. 1955. *Personal Influence.* New York: Free Press.

Kelley, Harold H., John W. Thibaut, Roland Radloff, and David Mundy. 1962. The Development of Cooperation in the "Minimal Social Situation." *Psychological Monographs* 76, no. 19: 538.

Kidder, Tracy. 1981. *The Soul of a New Machine.* Boston: Little, Brown.

Kontopoulos, Kyriakos M. 1993. Neural networks as a model of structure. In *The Logics of Social Structure*, 243–67. New York: Cambridge University Press.

Kowalski, Thaddeus J., and Leon S. Levy. 1996. *Rule-Based Programming.* Dordrecht, Netherlands: Kluwer.

Kurzweil, Ray. 1999. *The Age of Spiritual Machines.* New York: Penguin.

LaBarre, Weston. 1972. *The Ghost Dance.* New York: Dell.

Lanchester, Frederick William. 1956. Mathematics in Warfare. In *The World of Mathematics*, edited by James R. Newman, 2138–57. New York: Simon & Schuster.

Land, Kenneth C., Glenn Deane, and Judith R. Blau. 1991. Religious Pluralism and Church Membership: A Spatial Diffusion Model. *American Sociological Review* 56:237–49.

Leik, Robert K., and Barbara F. Meeker. 1995. Computer Simulation for Exploring Theories: Models of Interpersonal Cooperation and Competition. *Sociological Perspectives* 38:463–82.

Lévi-Strauss, Claude. 1963. The Sorcerer and His Magic. In *Structural Anthropology*, edited by Claude Lévi-Strauss, 161–80. New York: Basic Books.

Lewis, Ioan M. 1971. *Ecstatic Religion.* Baltimore: Penguin.

Lindner, Eileen W., ed. 2004. *Yearbook of American and Canadian Churches.* Nashville, Tenn.: Abingdon.

Lofland, John. 1966. *Doomsday Cult.* Englewood Cliffs, N.J.: Prentice-Hall.

Lofland, John, and Rodney Stark. 1965. Becoming a World-Saver: A Theory of Conversion to a Deviant Perspective. *American Sociological Review* 30:862–75.

Lynd, Robert S., and Helen Merrell Lynd. 1929. *Middletown.* New York: Harcourt, Brace.

———. 1937. *Middletown in Transition.* New York: Harcourt, Brace.

Macy, Michael W. 1995. PAVLOV and the Evolution of Cooperation: An Experimental Test. *Social Psychology Quarterly* 58:74–87.

Macy, Michael W., and John Skvoretz. 1998. The Evolution of Trust and Cooperation between Strangers: A Computational Model. *American Sociological Review* 63: 638–60.

Macy, Michael W., and R. Willer. 2002. From Factors to Actors: Computational Sociology and Agent-based Modeling. *Annual Review of Sociology* 28:143–66.

Mandelbrot, Benoit B. 1983. *The Fractal Geometry of Nature.* San Francisco: W. H. Freeman.

Mark, Noah. 1998. Beyond Individual Differences: Social Differentiation for First Principles. *American Sociological Review* 63:309–30.

Markovsky, Barry. 1992. Network Exchange Outcomes: Limits of Predictability. *Social Networks* 14:267–86.

Maynard Smith, John. 1982. *Evolution and the Theory of Games.* New York: Cambridge University Press.

Mayr, Ernst. 1964. *Systematics and the Origin of Species.* New York: Dover.

McKay, C. P. 1982. Terraforming Mars. *Journal of the British Interplanetary Society* 35:427–33.

Merton, Robert K. 1968. Social Structure and Anomie. In *Social Theory and Social Structure,* 185–214. New York: Free Press. (Originally published in 1938)

Messing, Simon D. 1958. Group Therapy and Social Status in the Zar Cult of Ethiopia. *American Anthropologist* 60:1120–26.

Miller, Neil E., and John Dollard. 1941. *Social Learning and Imitation.* New Haven, Conn.: Yale University Press.

Minsky, Marvin, and Seymour Papert. 1969. *Perceptrons.* Cambridge: MIT Press.

Moreno, Jacob. 1934. *Who Shall Survive?* Washington, D.C.: Nervous and Mental Disease Publishing.

Moretti, Sabrina. 2002. Computer Simulation in Sociology. *Social Science Computer Review* 20, no. 1: 43–57.

Newberg, Andrew, Eugene d'Aquili, and Vince Rause. 2001. *Why God Won't Go Away.* New York: Ballantine.

Nordhoff, Charles. 1875. *Communistic Societies of the United States.* London: John Murray.

Nowak, Martin, and Karl Sigmund. 1993. A Strategy of Win-Stay, Lose-Shift That Outperforms Tit-for-tat in the Prisoner's Dilemma Game. *Nature* 364:56–58.

Nuxoll, Andrew, and John E. Laird. 2004. A Cognitive Model of Episodic Memory Integrated with a General Cognitive Architecture. Paper presented at the International Conference on Cognitive Modeling. Available at ai.eecs.umich.edu/people/laird/papers/nuxoll-2004-ICCM-epmem.pdf (accessed 20 September 2005).

Perlis, Don. 2000. The Role(s) of Belief in AI. In *Logic-Based Artificial Intelligence,* edited by Jack Minter, 361–74. Boston: Kluwer.

Pinker, Steven. 1997. *How the Mind Works.* New York: Norton.

Quinlan, Philip T., ed. 2003. *Connectionist Models of Development: Developmental Processes in Real and Artificial Neural Networks.* New York: Psychology Press.

Rapoport, Anatol. 1962. The Use and Misuse of Game Theory. In *Mathematics in the Modern World,* edited by Morris Kline, 304–12. San Francisco: Freeman.

Rapoport, Anatol, and Albert M. Chammah. 1965. *Prisoner's Dilemma: A Study in Conflict and Cooperation.* Ann Arbor: University of Michigan Press.

Richardson, James T., Mary White Stewart, and Robert B. Simmonds. 1979. *Organized Miracles.* New Brunswick, N.J.: Transaction.

Robinson, Kim Stanley. 1993. *Red Mars.* New York: Bantam.

———. 1994. *Green Mars.* New York: Bantam.

———. 1996. *Blue Mars.* New York: Bantam.

Roco, Mihail C., and William Sims Bainbridge. 2002. *Converging Technologies for Improving Human Performance.* Dordrecht, Netherlands: Kluwer.

Roco, Mihail C., and Carlo D. Montemagno, eds. 2004. *The Coevolution of Human Potential and Converging Technologies.* New York: New York Academy of Sciences (Annals of the New York Academy of Sciences, volume 1013).

Rogers, Everett M. 1960. *Social Change in Rural Society.* New York: Appleton-Century-Crofts.

———. 1995. *Diffusion of Innovations.* New York: Free Press.

Roheim, Geza. 1955. *Magic and Schizophrenia.* Bloomington: Indiana University Press.

Rokeach, Milton. 1960. *The Open and Closed Mind.* New York: Basic Books.

Rothlisberger, F. J., and W. J. Dickson. 1939. *Management and the Worker.* Cambridge, Mass.: Harvard University Press.

Rumelhart, D. E., and J. L. McClelland. 1986. *Parallel Distributed Processing.* Cambridge: MIT Press.

Russell, Stuart, and Peter Norvig. 1995. *Artificial Intelligence: A Modern Approach.* Upper Saddle River, N.J.: Prentice Hall.

Schelling, Thomas C. 1960. *The Strategy of Conflict.* Cambridge, Mass.: Harvard University Press.

———. 1978. *Micromotives and Macrobehavior.* New York: Norton.

Schultz, Thomas R. 2003. *Computational Developmental Psychology.* Cambridge, Mass.: MIT Press.

Scott, John Finley. 1971. *Internalization of Norms.* Englewood Cliffs, N.J.: Prentice-Hall.

Shastri, Lokendra. 2001. A Computational Model of Episodic Memory Formation in the Hippocampal System. *Neurocomputing* 38–40:889–97.

———. 2002. Episodic Memory and Cortico-hippocampal Interactions. *Trends in Cognitive Sciences* 6:162–68.

Sidowski, Joseph B., Benjamin Wyckoff, and Leon Tabory. 1956. The Influence of Reinforcement and Punishment in a Minimal Social Situation. *Journal of Abnormal and Social Psychology* 52:115–19.

Silverman, Julian. 1967. Shamans and Acute Schizophrenia. *American Anthropologist* 69:21–32.

Simpson, John H. 1990. The Stark-Bainbridge Theory of Religion. *Journal for Scientific Study of Religion* 29:367–71.

Skinner, B. F. 1938. *The Behavior of Organisms.* New York: Appleton-Century.

Skvoretz, John, Thomas J. Fararo, and Filip Agneessens. 2004. Advances in Biased Net Theory: Definitions, Derivations, and Estimations. *Social Networks* 26:113–39.

Smelser, Neil J. 1962. *Theory of Collective Behavior.* New York: Free Press.

Smith, Murray. 1993. *Neural Networks for Statistical Modeling.* New York: Van Nostrand.

Smith, Thomas S., and Gregory T. Stevens. 1999. The Architecture of Small Networks: Strong Interaction and Dynamic Organization in Small Social Systems. *American Sociological Review* 64:403–20.

Spengler, Oswald. 1926. *The Decline of the West.* New York: Knopf.

Stark, Rodney. 1996a. *The Rise of Christianity.* Princeton, N.J.: Princeton University Press.

———. 1996b. Why Religious Movement Succeed or Fail: A Revised General Model. *Journal of Contemporary Religion* 11:133–46.

Stark, Rodney, and William Sims Bainbridge. 1979. Of Churches, Sects, and Cults: Preliminary Concepts for a Theory of Religious Movements. *Journal for the Scientific Study of Religion* 18:117–31.

———. 1980a. Networks of Faith: Interpersonal Bonds and Recruitment to Cults and Sects. *American Journal of Sociology* 85, no. 6: 1376–95.

———. 1980b. Towards a Theory of Religion: Religious Commitment. *Journal for the Scientific Study of Religion* 19:114–28.

———. 1985. *The Future of Religion.* Berkeley: University of California Press.

———. 1987. *A Theory of Religion.* New York: Lang & Toronto Studies in Religion.

———. 1996. *Religion, Deviance, and Social Control.* New York: Routledge.

Stark, Rodney, and Roger Finke. 1988. Religious Economies and Sacred Canopies. *American Sociological Review* 53:41–49.

———. 2000. *Acts of Faith.* Berkeley: University of California Press.

Stark, Rodney, and Lynne Roberts. 1982. The Arithmetic of Social Movements: Theoretical Implications. *Sociological Analysis* 43:53–68.

Stein, Dan J., and Jacques Lidik, eds. 1998. *Neural Networks and Psychopathology.* Cambridge: Cambridge University Press.

Sutherland, Edwin H. 1947. *Principles of Criminology.* Philadelphia: Lippincott.

Takahashi, Nobuyuku. 2000. The Emergence of Generalized Exchange. *American Journal of Sociology* 105:1105–34.

Thrasher, Frederic M. 1927. *The Gang.* Chicago, Ill.: University of Chicago Press.

Turkle, Sherry. 1995. *Life on the Screen.* New York: Simon & Schuster.

von Braun, Wernher, 1953. *The Mars Project.* Urbana: University of Illinois Press.

Wallace, Anthony F. C. 1956. Revitalization Movements. *American Anthropologist* 58:264–81.

Warner, Philip. 1985. *Kitchener: The Man behind the Legend.* London: Hamish Hamilton.

Warner, R. S. 1993. Work in Progress toward a New Paradigm for the Sociological Study of Religion in the United States. *American Journal of Sociology* 98:1044–93.

Warner, W. Lloyd, and Paul S. Lunt. 1941. *The Social Life of a Modern Community.* New Haven, Conn.: Yale University Press.

Wasserman, Philip D. 1989. *Neural Computing: Theory and Practice.* New York: Van Nostrand Reinhold.

———. 1993. *Advanced Methods in Neural Computing.* New York: Van Nostrand.

Watson, Helen. 1990. Investigating the Social Foundations of Mathematics: Natural Number in Culturally Diverse Forms of Life. *Social Studies of Science* 20:283–312.

Watts, Duncan J. 1999. Networks, Dynamics, and the Small World Problem. *American Journal of Sociology* 105:493–527.

Whitehouse, Harvey. 2004. *Modes of Religiosity.* Walnut Creek, Calif.: AltaMira.

Whitehouse, Harvey, and James Laidlaw, eds. 2004. *Ritual and Memory: Toward a Comparative Anthropology of Religion.* Walnut Creek, Calif.: AltaMira.

Whitehouse, Harvey, and Luther H. Martin, eds. 2004. *Theorizing Religions Past: Archaeology, History, and Cognition.* Walnut Creek, Calif.: AltaMira.

Wilson, Edward O. 1975. *Sociobiology: The New Synthesis.* Cambridge, Mass.: Belknap Press of Harvard University Press.

Xenophon. 1998. *Anabasis.* Cambridge, Mass.: Harvard University Press.

Zipf, George Kingsley. 1949. *Human Behavior and the Principle of Least Effort.* Cambridge, Mass.: Addison-Wesley Press.

Zubrin, Robert. 1996. *The Case for Mars.* New York: Free Press.

Index

About the Author

William Sims Bainbridge earned his doctorate in sociology from Harvard University and is the author of eleven books, four textbook-software packages, and about two hundred shorter publications in the social science of religion, information science, and technology. He has published extensively on new religious movements, including the general textbook, *The Sociology of Religious Movements* (1997), and sociological case studies of two movements: *Satan's Power* (1978) and *The Endtime Family* (2002). With Rodney Stark, he wrote three books outlining a general social-scientific approach to religion: *The Future of Religion* (1985), *A Theory of Religion* (1987), and *Religion, Deviance and Social Control* (1996). His software employed innovative techniques to teach theory and methodology: *Experiments in Psychology* (1986), *Sociology Laboratory* (1987), *Survey Research* (1989), and *Social Research Methods and Statistics* (1992). Among very recent projects are editing *The Encyclopedia of Human Computer Interaction* (2004) and co-editing *Societal Implications of Nanoscience and Nanotechnology* (2001), *Converging Technologies for Improving Human Performance* (2003), *Nanotechnology: Societal Implications—Improving Benefits for Humanity* (2005), and *Managing Nano-Bio-Info-Cogno Innovations: Converging Technologies in Society* (2006).